G000253593

Thomson Round Hall Nutshells

Evidence

Round Hall Nutshells

Evidence

Ross Gorman
B.A., B.L.

<small>SERIES EDITOR</small>
Bruce Carolan

ROUND HALL

 THOMSON REUTERS

Published in 2006 by
Thomson Reuters (Professional) Ireland Limited
(Registered in Ireland, Company No. 80867. Registered Office
and address for service 43 Fitzwilliam Place, Dublin 2)
trading as Round Hall.

Typeset by
Siobhan Mullholland

Printed by Clays Ltd, St Ives plc

ISBN 978-1-85800-421-1

A catalogue record for this book is available from the British Library.

All rights reserved. No part of this publication may be reproduced or transmitted
in any form or by any means, or stored in any retrieval system of any nature
without prior written permission. Such written permission must also be obtained
before any part of this publication is stored in a retrieval system of any nature.

Thomson Reuters and the Thomson Reuters Logo are trademarks of
Thomson Reuters. Round Hall is a registered trademark of Thomson Reuters
(Professional) Ireland Limited.

© 2006 Thomson Reuters (Professional) Ireland Limited

To my Parents

Acknowledgments

I would like to thank a number of people who helped me with this work. I would like to thank Carol Gaffney for volunteering to type some of the book. I would like to express my gratitude to David McCartney, formerly of Thomson Round Hall, for his enthusiasm for this project. I am particularly grateful to Susan Rossney, the commissioning editor in Thomson Round Hall, for her unfailing good humour and patience. Finally, I would like to thank the legal editor Suzanna Henry and the copyeditor Orla Fee.

Table of Contents

TABLE OF LEGISLATION

CONSTITUTION OF IRELAND

IRISH ACTS

ENGLISH LEGISLATION

EUROPEAN LEGISLATION

STATUTORY INSTRUMENTS

RULES OF COURT

TABLE OF CASES

TABLE OF IRISH CASES

TABLE OF UK CASES

TABLE OF EUROPEAN CASES

1. INTRODUCTION

1.1 RELEVANCE

This book is mainly concerned with the legal rules that determine whether evidence is admissible in a particular case. According to Hardiman J. in *People (DPP) v O'Callaghan* ([2001] 1 I.R. 584) "relevance is the first and most basic requirement of admissibility".

Therefore, the starting point for determining the admissibility of evidence is whether it is relevant. The most frequently cited definition of relevance is that given by Sir James Stephen in his *Digest of the Law of Evidence*. He stated that

> "any two facts to which it is applied are so related to each other that according to the common course of events one either taken by itself or in connection with other facts proves or renders probable the past, present, or future existence or non-existence of the other."

Similarly in *DPP v Kilbourne* ([1973] A.C. 729) Lord Simon in the House of Lords stated that:

> "Evidence is relevant if it is logically probative or disprobative of some matter which requires proof...relevant (*i.e.* logically probative or disprobative) evidence is evidence which makes the matter which requires proof more or less probable."

However, just because evidence is relevant does not automatically mean it is admissible. In fact, as irrelevant evidence is never admissible, the laws of evidence are generally concerned with when relevant evidence should be excluded. This has led to them being described as exclusionary rules.

For the most part the rules of evidence are concerned with the criminal trial. This is because common law judges concerned with ensuring the accused received a fair trial developed many of these rules. This rationale is also evident in more modern times. In *People (AG) v O'Brien* ([1965] I.R. 142) Walsh J. noted: "the primary purpose of the rules of evidence is to ensure a fair trial of the person accused". This is understandable given the severe consequences for an accused if he is found guilty. For this reason this book inevitably focuses on the criminal trial. In fact it will be seen that some rules of

1

evidence are inapplicable to a civil trial, *e.g.* the right to silence of an accused, while the litigants in civil cases frequently waive other rules of evidence, *e.g.* the rule against hearsay.

2. THE BURDEN OF PROOF

2.1 INTRODUCTION

This chapter will begin by examining the meaning of the phrase "the burden of proof". Subsequently it will explore who bears this burden in legal proceedings. Finally it will analyse what standard of proof is required to satisfy this burden. All of these issues will be considered in relation to both criminal and civil litigation.

2.2 THE MEANING OF THE "BURDEN OF PROOF"

The best way of understanding the phrase "burden of proof" is to regard it as being made up of two distinct concepts—a legal burden and an evidential burden. Approaching it in this way makes it easier to understand the court's approach to situations when the burden of proof shifts.

2.2.1 The legal burden of proof

This can be regarded as the burden of proof proper. It is the obligation placed on a party to satisfy the judge or jury in relation to a particular fact. If someone bears the legal burden of proof in a case he must persuade the judge or jury to the requisite standard of proof, or else he will lose the case.

2.2.2 The evidential burden of proof

A party who bears an evidential burden of proof must make out a prima facie case. They must put forward sufficient evidence so that it is possible for them to succeed. In criminal cases or a civil case with a jury the evidential burden is satisfied when the party on whom it is placed puts forward enough evidence to prevent the trial judge withdrawing the case from the jury. In such cases the jury decides if the legal burden is satisfied but the judge decides if the evidential burden is.

2.3 THE BURDEN OF PROOF IN CRIMINAL CASES

Generally in criminal cases the burden of proof is on the prosecution. The accused is presumed to be innocent unless the prosecution prove otherwise. One of the most famous enunciations of this principle was the House of Lord's decision in *Woolmington v DPP* ([1935] A.C. 462). The accused's wife left him and went to live with her

3

mother. He went to visit her to persuade her to come back and immediately after he left a neighbour discovered her dead body. She had been shot in the heart. The accused was charged with murder. He admitted shooting her; however, he maintained it was an accident. He claimed that she had refused to return and he said that if she did not he would kill himself. At that point he raised the gun to show what he intended to do but it went off accidentally, killing her.

In his direction to the jury the trial judge gave them the impression that once the prosecution proved that the accused killed the deceased they should convict him of murder unless he could prove he was not guilty. The House of Lords disapproved of this direction saying it is not for an accused to establish his innocence, rather the prosecution must establish his guilt. Viscount Sankey L.C. famously stated:

> "Throughout the web of the English Criminal Law one golden thread is always to be seen, that it is the duty of the prosecution to prove the prisoner's guilt subject to what I have already said as to the defence of insanity and subject also to any statutory exception…No matter what the charge or where the trial, the principle that the prosecution must prove the guilt of the prisoner is part of the common law of England and no attempt to whittle it down can be entertained."

This statement has been approved in this jurisdiction on numerous occasions. For example in *People (AG) v McMahon* ([1946] I.R. 267) Maguire P. referred to the ruling in *Woolmington* and said: "[t]he Court is of the opinion that this principle is the true one, and, as applicable to the facts of this case, imposes on the prosecution the necessity of negativing every supposition consistent with the innocence of the accused."

2.3.1 Exceptions to the rule in *Woolmington*

There are several exceptions to the principle set out in *Woolmington*. Indeed, Viscount Shankey L.C. recognised this in the above quotation when he noted that the principle he had outlined was subject to the defence of insanity and to statutory exceptions.

(i) Insanity

Every accused is presumed to be sane. In *R v M'Naghten* ((1843) 4 St. Tr. 847) the House of Lords established that the legal burden of establishing the defence of insanity rests upon the accused. This decision was expressly approved in Ireland in *AG v Boylan* ([1937] I.R. 449). However, an accused only has to prove this defence to the civil standard of proof (on the balance of probabilities).

(ii) Statutory exceptions

Several statutes appear to place the burden of proof on the accused. The constitutionality of such provisions has been challenged in a number of cases. The objection taken in these cases is that this shift in the burden of proof is contrary to the presumption of innocence. In rejecting this argument the courts have focused on the distinction between a legal burden of proof and an evidential one noted earlier.

The leading judgment in this jurisdiction is the decision of Costello J. in *O'Leary v AG* ([1991] I.L.R.M. 454). Here the applicant was convicted in the Special Criminal Court of membership of an unlawful organisation contrary to s.21 of the Offences Against the State Act 1939 and of having in his possession incriminating documents contrary to s.12 of the 1939 Act. He then instituted these proceedings seeking a declaration that the two statutory provisions used to secure his earlier conviction were unconstitutional because they were contrary to the presumption of innocence. The sections were s.3(2) of the Offences Against the State (Amendment) Act 1972 and s.24 of the 1939 Act. Costello J. began by noting that the phrase "the burden of proof" has two entirely different meanings. Therefore, in any case where it was claimed that the burden of proof shifted to the accused it was important to examine the wording of the statute to see whether it was the legal or the evidential burden that shifted. It is only when a statute places the legal burden on an accused that it might be unconstitutional. If the evidential burden is all that shifts then no question of unconstitutionality arises as the legal burden of proof is still on the prosecution.

He then analysed the two provisions in question. Section 3(2) of the 1972 Act provides that where a garda not below the rank of chief superintendent states that he believes that the accused was a member of an unlawful organisation, that statement is evidence that he was such a member. Costello J. held that this section did not effect an accused's presumption of innocence in any way. All it did was to make admissible statements of belief which would otherwise be inadmissible.

Section 24 of the 1939 Act provides that proof of possession by an accused of an incriminating document shall, without more, be evidence until the contrary is proved that he was a member of the unlawful organisation. Costello J. held that this section only shifts an evidential burden onto the accused. It did not oblige an accused to give evidence so as to avoid a conviction. To do this the section would have to be worded differently. Instead it allowed the court to evaluate the significance of the document tendered and to draw inferences from its possession by the accused. The extent of the inferences that could be drawn would vary depending on the document found and the circumstances of its discovery. Therefore, a statute that permits a court to evaluate the significance of the document and find that an accused is not guilty without any exculpatory evidence tendered on his behalf could not be contrary to the presumption of innocence. Consequently he refused the application. The Supreme Court upheld this judgment.

A similar conclusion was reached in *Hardy v Ireland* ([1994] 2 I.R. 550). Here the court was considering s.4(1) of the Explosive Substances Act 1883. This section provides that any person who knowingly has an explosive substance is his possession, under such circumstances as to give rise to a reasonable suspicion that he does not have it in his possession for a lawful object, shall be guilty of a felony unless he can show that he had it in his possession for a lawful object. In the High Court Flood J. held that this subsection was compatible with an accused's constitutional right to trial in due course of law under Art.38.1 of the Constitution as all it did was place an evidential burden of proof on the accused. The legal burden of proof still remained on the prosecution.

A majority of the Supreme Court upheld this decision. They felt that there were two aspects to the subsection. First, the prosecution had to establish beyond reasonable doubt circumstances of reasonable suspicion that the accused did not have the explosives in his possession for a lawful object. If the prosecution did this then the accused had to satisfy an evidential burden that he did have them in his possession for a lawful purpose. The minority felt that the second half of the subsection did place a legal burden on the accused to prove a lawful object. However, this did not mean that the subsection was unconstitutional. There was nothing in the Constitution that absolutely prohibited a statute shifting the legal burden onto an accused. This was especially true here because the shift only occurred after the prosecution had established a reasonable suspicion. In so holding Murphy J. emphasised that it was very difficult for the prosecution to obtain a conviction for these types of crimes.

(iii) The peculiar knowledge principle

Historically the peculiar knowledge principle was regarded as the third exception to the rule in *Woolmington*. However, it is debatable whether this exception still exists. The principle provided that where a fact is peculiarly within the knowledge of the defendant the legal burden of proof in relation to that fact was on the defendant and not the prosecution.

Initially the courts in Ireland were prepared to make use of this principle. In *Minister for Industry and Commerce v Steele* ([1952] I.R. 304) the accused was convicted in the District Court of breaches of the Emergency Powers (Pork Sausages and Sausage Meat) (Maximum Prices) Order 1943. This order defined pork sausages as sausages not less than 65 per cent of the meat content of which consisted of pork. An employee of the complainant bought some sausages from the accused and he was issued with a receipt which described them as pork sausages. The accused appealed his conviction claiming there was no evidence that the sausages he sold were pork sausages, that the burden of proof was on the complainant and that they had not discharged this burden. The complainant maintained that the receipt the defendant issued to their employee describing the sausages as pork sausages was proof. Furthermore, there was no evidence that the meat in the sausages was anything other than pork; if there was any meat other than pork in the sausages that was a matter peculiarly within the knowledge of the defendant and therefore he bore the burden of proof. The Circuit Court judge accepted that it was not possible to prove by analysis what percentage of the meat content of the sausages was pork. However, he allowed the appeal as the complainant had failed to discharge the burden of proof. At the request of the complainant he stated a case to the Supreme Court on the issue.

The Supreme Court held that in the circumstances the burden of proof had shifted to the accused because the matter was peculiarly within his knowledge. Murnaghan J. noted that as it was impossible to prove what percentage of the meat content was pork, to hold that the burden had not shifted would make a conviction impossible. Therefore, the trial judge had been correct to hold that the sausages were pork sausages within the meaning of the order.

However, the High Court and Supreme Court judgments in *McGowan v Carville* ([1960] I.R. 330) make clear that the courts were becoming uneasy with relying on this peculiar knowledge principle. The accused was driving a van and was stopped by the complainant garda. He was asked to produce his driver's licence. He could not, but he indicated that he would produce it at a garda station. Subsequently the accused was charged with driving without a licence contrary to s.22(1) of the Road Traffic Act 1933. He did not appear at the District Court and was not represented. The complaint was heard in his absence. No evidence was given as to whether or not the accused had produced his licence at a garda station. The District Justice felt that the burden of proof was on the complainant, that he had failed to discharge this burden and, therefore, he dismissed the complaint.

On the application of the complainant the District Justice stated a case to the High Court as to whether he was correct. In the High Court Davitt P. began by emphasising the general rule that the burden of proving every constituent element of an offence was on the prosecution. He accepted that in certain circumstances this could make a conviction impossible and in such circumstances the burden of proof could shift to an accused. But it was only in these limited circumstances that the peculiar knowledge principle could apply. He also suggested that the word peculiarly should be taken to mean "exclusively" or "almost exclusively". In the case at hand he held that the principle should not be applied and the burden of proof should remain on the complainant. He concluded by suggesting that if it had been established that the accused had not gone to a garda station then perhaps the burden of proof would have shifted. The Supreme Court upheld this judgment.

Davitt P. considered the peculiar knowledge principle again in *AG v Shorten* ([1961] I.R. 304). Here the accused was charged with having made a declaration that he, or someone with his consent, had not used his car for four months, for the purpose of obtaining a licence, knowing that declaration to be false or misleading. The prosecution's case was that two gardaí had seen the car being driven during the period covered by the declaration. However, the gardaí could not identify the driver of the car. When the accused was interviewed by the gardaí he said he could offer no explanation, as he believed his declaration to be true. Later he claimed that he was not at home on the night in question and that the car was there when he left and when he returned the following day. The defence applied to have the case dismissed, but the District Judge refused as he felt that once the use of the car had been established, the burden of proof had shifted to the accused.

A case was stated to the High Court. Davitt P. reiterated his dissatisfaction with the peculiar knowledge principle. He stated: "I find it very hard to regard resort to the 'peculiar knowledge' principle, even in its modified form, or any similar principle, as other than attempts to whittle down the principle of the presumption of innocence." Here there were other people (including family members) who could have driven the car without the accused's knowledge; therefore, he held that the burden of proof had not shifted to the accused.

The principle has also proved unpopular in the UK. In *R v Edwards* ([1975] Q.B. 27) Lawton L.J. in the Court of Appeal pointed out that an accused's intention is something which could be said to be peculiarly within his knowledge. Therefore, applying the rule could force an accused charged with an offence that requires intention to be present to prove that they did not intend to commit the crime. This would in effect require them to prove their innocence.

2.4 CIVIL CASES AND THE BURDEN OF PROOF

Obviously, in civil litigation rules like the presumption of innocence have no application. Instead the general rule is that the party who asserts a fact must prove it. This could be the plaintiff or the defendant. For example, in a negligence claim the plaintiff must prove the existence of a duty of care, breach of that duty by the defendant and that he suffered damage as a result of the breach. If the defendant claims that the plaintiff was guilty of contributory negligence he must prove that. However, there are exceptions to this general rule. The most important exception is the doctrine of *res ipsa loquitur*.

2.4.1 *Res ipsa loquitur*

This phrase literally means: "the acts speak for themselves". The classic formulation of the doctrine was that set out in *Scott v London and St Katherine Docks Company* ([1861–73] All E.R. Rep. 246).

> "Where the thing is shown to be under the management of the defendant or his servants, and the accident is such as in the ordinary course of things does not happen if those who have the management use proper care, it affords reasonable evidence, in the absence of explanation by the defendants, that the accident arose from want of care."

In effect the rule shifts the burden of proof from the plaintiff on to the defendant. This doctrine has been applied in Ireland. For example, in *Mullen v Quinnsworth* ([1991] I.L.R.M. 439) the 74-year-old plaintiff slipped on vegetable oil on the floor of the defendants' supermarket. The Supreme Court held that the doctrine applied. Therefore, the burden of proof shifted to the defendants. They had to show that they were not negligent.

It was also applied in *Lindsay v Mid-Western Health Board* ([1993] I.L.R.M. 550). The defendant was in charge of the hospital the plaintiff was admitted to. The plaintiff had her appendix removed but she never regained consciousness after the operation. She suffered irreversible brain damage. The Supreme Court held that in such circumstances the doctrine of *res ipsa loquitur* applied.

However, it is worth noting that the Supreme Court also held that all the defendant had to do was establish that they had exercised all reasonable care and were not negligent in carrying out the operation. They did not have to prove what did cause the brain damage. This latter point, while controversial, is justified because it is more consistent with the underlying justification of the rule. The rule is designed to prevent unfairness. To require the defendant to prove what did happen would have been excessive and therefore unfair on the defendant.

This was the approach taken by Henchy J. in *Hanrahan v Merck, Sharpe and Dohme Ltd* ([1988] I.L.R.M. 629). He stated: "The rationale behind the shifting of the onus of proof to the defendant in such cases would appear to lie in the fact that it would be palpably unfair to require a plaintiff to prove something which is beyond his reach and which is peculiarly within the range of the defendant's *capacity of proof* [emphasis added]."

This limitation on the rule was controversial but it was approved by the Supreme Court in *Rothwell v Motor Insurers' Bureau of Ireland* ([2003] 1 I.R. 268). Here Hardiman J. said it was not enough that something was within the exclusive knowledge of the defendant, it also had to be "peculiarly within the range of the defendant's capacity for proof". The defendant is a body which is required to compensate a plaintiff who has been injured in a road traffic accident when the driver whose negligence caused the accident, *inter alia*, cannot be traced. In this case the plaintiff suffered personal injuries when his car skidded on an oil spill. As he could not prove that a negligent driver left the oil spill he sought to rely on the doctrine of *res ipsa loquitur*. The Supreme Court refused to permit the plaintiff to do this as the person who caused the spill was not within the defendant's capacity of proof.

2.5 THE STANDARD OF PROOF

2.5.1 Criminal cases

The prosecution must prove the guilt of the accused beyond reasonable doubt. Over the years there have been numerous attempts by the judiciary to clarify this phrase for jurors. Denning J. provided one of the most enduring explanations in *Miller v Minister of Pensions* ([1947] 2 All E.R. 372):

> "Proof beyond a reasonable doubt does not mean beyond the shadow of a doubt. The law would fail to protect the community if it admitted fanciful possibilities to deflect the course of justice. If the evidence is so strong against a man as to leave only a remote possibility in his favour, which can be dismissed with the sentence 'of course it is possible but not in the least probable' the case is proved beyond a reasonable doubt, but nothing short of that will suffice."

However, many of these so-called clarifications were criticised by appellate courts. In fact, in *R v Ching* ((1976) 63 Cr. App. R. 7) the English Court of Appeal commented: "If judges stopped trying to define that which is almost impossible to define, there would be fewer appeals." Therefore, it is now common for trial judges not to explain the phrase unless the jury asks for clarification. Instead the jurors are left to use their common sense.

In *AG v Byrne* ([1974] I.R. 1) Kenny J. held that it would be helpful to explain to jurors the strictness of the criminal standard of proof by contrasting it with the civil standard. However, the Court of Criminal Appeal in *People (DPP) v Shortt* (unreported, July 23, 1996) held that a trial judge is not obliged to do this.

If the burden of proof is on the accused, for example if he raises the defence of insanity, he only has to discharge it to the civil standard of proof (on the balance of probabilities).

2.5.2 Civil cases

Whoever bears the burden of proof in civil cases must satisfy the court on the balance of probabilities. In *Miller v Minister of Pensions* Denning J. described this standard as follows:

> "It must carry a reasonable degree of probability, but not so high as is required in a criminal case. If the evidence is such that the tribunal can say: 'We think it more probable than not,' the burden is discharged, but, if the probabilities are equal, it is not."

3. THE TESTIMONY OF WITNESSES

3.1 INTRODUCTION

Under our adversarial system one of the primary ways in which a party tries to prove its case is by the testimony of witnesses. This chapter will examine this process. First it will consider the competence and compellability of witnesses. It will then look at the evidential rules that apply during the examination-in-chief and cross-examination of witnesses. Next it will set out the circumstances in which previous consistent statements of witnesses can be referred to during their testimony. Finally, this chapter will consider whether witnesses can refer to notes before they testify or during their testimony and whether witnesses can give their evidence by a live television link instead of in the courtroom.

3.2 COMPETENCE AND COMPELLABILITY OF WITNESSES

3.2.1 Introduction

A witness is competent to testify if he is capable of giving evidence in court. A compellable witness is a competent witness who can be required to give evidence. In general at common law anyone who was capable of understanding the nature and consequences of an oath was competent to testify and all competent witnesses were compellable. However, a number of exceptions to these general rules have been developed. This section will examine the compellability of an accused and his or her spouse and whether children or witnesses with a mental disability are competent to testify.

3.2.2 Accused persons

At common law an accused was not a competent witness either for the defence or for the prosecution. This position was changed by s.1 of the Criminal Justice (Evidence) Act 1924, which provides that an accused is competent to testify on behalf of the defence if he wants to do so. An accused is still not competent to testify for the prosecution.

If an accused is charged jointly with another person he is a competent witness for his co-accused but he is not compellable; however, he is neither competent nor compellable for the prosecution. If a person ceases to be jointly charged with his co-accused he would then be competent and compellable on behalf of the

13

prosecution. This could happen where (a) he is acquitted; (b) he pleads guilty; (c) the prosecution enter a *nolle prosequi* against him; or (d) the trial judge severs the indictment so they are tried separately.

3.2.3 The spouse of the accused person

3.2.3.1 As a witness for the prosecution
There was a general common law rule that a spouse was not competent to testify for the prosecution. However, this rule did not apply if the accused was charged with certain acts of violence against his spouse. Section 4 of the Criminal Justice (Evidence) Act 1924 provided that a spouse was competent to testify for the prosecution if the accused was charged with any of a list of scheduled offences, *e.g.* if he was charged with an offence under the Offences Against the Person Act 1861.

In *People (DPP) v J.T.* ((1988) 3 Frewen 141) Walsh J. in the Court of Criminal Appeal questioned the validity of this general rule. He stated: "It could strongly be argued that this rule...could only be regarded as outmoded and unreal." Here the appellant was convicted of a number of sexual offences against his daughter. The accused's spouse testified for the prosecution during his trial. On appeal the defence claimed that to permit the spouse to testify against her husband was contrary to the protection guaranteed to the family by Art.41 of the Constitution.

Walsh J. rejected this argument. He stated that it was not intended that one family member could use Art.41 to escape punishment for an assault on another family member. He held that as Art.41 required the courts to protect the family and that as the offences here were "an attack on the very fabric of the family", the courts were required to allow the spouse to testify. In fact he suggested that a spouse could be compelled to testify in such circumstances.

This judgment was one of the reasons for the introduction of the Criminal Justice Evidence Act 1992. Section 21 of the 1992 Act makes a spouse or former spouse competent to give evidence for the prosecution in any criminal proceedings (unless the spouse is a co-accused). Section 22 of the Act makes a spouse compellable for the prosecution, but only if the offence:

1) involves violence (or threatened violence) against the spouse, a child of the spouse or the accused, or anyone who was under 17 at the material time; or

2) is a sexual offence allegedly committed against a child of the spouse or the accused, or anyone who was under 17 at the material time; or
3) consists of attempting, or conspiring to commit, or of aiding, abetting, counselling, procuring or inciting the commission of either of the above offences.

3.2.3.2 As a witness for the accused

At common law a spouse was not competent to testify for the accused. This was because the law regarded them as one and the accused was not permitted to testify.

Section 1 of the Criminal Justice (Evidence) Act 1924 provided that a spouse was competent but not compellable on behalf of the accused. The 1992 Act now provides that a spouse or former spouse is both competent and compellable as a witness for the accused.

3.2.4 Children

At common law children were competent to give evidence once they could give sworn evidence. In other words, children had to understand the nature and consequences of an oath before they could testify. This position has been changed by legislation, which permits children to give unsworn evidence. The Criminal Evidence Act 1992 deals with the competency of children in criminal cases. Section 27(1) of the 1992 Act provides that in criminal proceedings a child under 14 may give evidence otherwise than on oath if the court is satisfied that he is capable of giving an intelligible account of the relevant events. The Children Act 1997 deals with the competency of children in civil cases. Section 28(1) of that Act is in almost identical terms to s.27(1) of the 1992 Act. It provides that a child under 14 may give evidence otherwise than on oath if the court is satisfied that he is capable of giving an intelligible account of the relevant events.

3.2.5 Persons with a mental disability

Persons of any age with a mental disability also have to satisfy the requirements set out in s.27(1) of the Criminal Evidence Act 1992 (in criminal trials) and s.28(1) of the Children Act 1997 (in civil cases).

3.2.6 Diplomats

Section 5(1) of the Diplomatic Relations Immunities Act 1967 incorporates the Vienna Convention on Diplomatic Relations into Irish law. This convention provides that diplomatic agents, members of administrative and technical staff of the mission, as well as their non-national families, are not obliged to give evidence as witnesses in either criminal or civil proceedings.

3.3 THE EXAMINATION-IN-CHIEF

The examination-in-chief is when the party that calls the witness asks him questions. The two main evidential rules that will be considered under this heading are the prohibition on asking leading questions and the rules regarding hostile witnesses.

3.3.1 Leading questions

In general a witness may not be asked a leading question during the examination-in-chief. A leading question is a question in which the answer is suggested. For example the question "was it raining that day?" is a leading question, but "what was the weather like that day?" is not. The reason for the rule is so that the witness gives his evidence in his own words and not the words suggested by counsel. However, there are a number of exceptions to this rule. It is common for a witness to be asked leading questions at the beginning of their testimony about non-contentious matters. For example, a witness may be led through the evidence of his name, address and occupation, etc. Witnesses may also be asked leading questions if the trial judge declares the witness to be hostile.

3.3.2 Hostile witnesses

Normally the party that calls a witness cannot cross-examine him or attack his credibility. So if a witness does not give the evidence he was expected to, very little can be done. However, if the witness goes further and starts telling lies or refuses to answer questions, the party who called him can apply to the trial judge (in the absence of the jury) to have him declared a hostile witness. If this application is granted the witness can be cross-examined, he can be asked leading questions and previous inconsistent statements can be put to him. The common law rules in relation to hostile witnesses have been supplemented by the Criminal Procedure Act 1865. Section 3 of that Act (which also applies to civil proceedings), provides that:

> "A party producing a witness shall not be allowed to impeach his credit by general evidence of bad character, but he may, in case the witness shall, in the opinion of the judge, prove adverse [now taken to mean hostile], contradict him by other evidence, or, by leave of the judge, prove that he has made at other times a statement inconsistent with his present testimony".

3.4 CROSS-EXAMINATION

After the examination-in-chief a witness can be cross-examined by the other side. During cross-examination the witness may be asked leading questions. One of the main reasons why witnesses are cross-examined is to undermine their previous testimony. Therefore, during cross-examination witnesses can be subject to fairly rigorous questioning. This is a necessary part of an adversarial system of justice. However, certain limitations must be placed on cross-examinations, otherwise a trial could be delayed indefinitely. One such limitation is the collateral issue rule.

3.4.1 The collateral issue rule

This rule provides that once a witness answers a question during cross-examination on a collateral issue, that answer is final and no evidence may be adduced to contradict it. It is consequently important to establish what is meant by a collateral issue. In *Attorney-General v Hitchcock* ((1847) 1 Exch. 91) it was held that if the cross-examining party would be allowed to prove the matter when they were giving evidence, because it was connected with the issues in the case, then the issue could not be regarded as collateral. It was also suggested that a collateral issue relates to the credibility of a witness rather than a fact in issue in the case.

There are a number of exceptions to the collateral issue rule where the cross-examining party can rebut the evidence tendered in answer to a collateral question. Five such exceptions will be considered here: (a) previous inconsistent statements; (b) previous convictions; (c) evidence of bias; (d) evidence of the untruthfulness of a witness; (e) a physical or mental disability of a witness.

3.4.1.1 Previous inconsistent statements

A witness can be cross-examined about statements he made prior to the trial which are inconsistent with his testimony in the trial. Sections 4 and 5 of the Criminal Procedure Act 1865 govern this exception. If the witness accepts that he made an inconsistent statement, then his credibility has been undermined and that is the end of the matter. However, if he denies having made the statement then it may be proved in evidence against him.

3.4.1.2 Previous convictions

Under s.6 of the Criminal Procedure Act 1865 a witness may be questioned about his previous convictions, even if this is a collateral issue. However, if the defence rely on this provision in a criminal trial the accused may expose himself to cross-examination on his own previous convictions under s.1(f) of the Criminal Justice (Evidence) Act 1924. This will be considered in more detail in chapter 7.

3.4.1.3 Bias

If a witness denies that he is biased then the party cross-examining him may introduce evidence to rebut this denial. In *People (DPP) v McGinley* ([1987] I.R. 340) the appellant was convicted of larceny. The main prosecution witness was an accomplice. Counsel for the appellant had attempted to cross-examine the accomplice about what happened at his trial to show that he had received a suspended sentence because he gave an undertaking to co-operate in the prosecution of the appellant. The trial judge ruled that this was a collateral issue and therefore the defence were bound by the answers given by the accomplice. The Court of Criminal Appeal ordered a re-trial because the questioning fell "within the general category of questioning seeking to lead to the establishing of partiality, bias or improper motive on the part of the witness, as distinct from a general assertion of lack of credit".

3.4.1.4 A witness's untruthfulness

A witness may testify that in his opinion another witness is not telling the truth. However, he cannot give evidence of the facts on which this belief is based.

3.4.1.5 A witness's physical or mental disability

Evidence of a witness's physical or mental disability may be tendered in evidence to show that his testimony is unreliable. In *Toohey v*

Metropolitan Police Commissioner ([1965] A.C. 595) the House of Lords accepted that evidence that a witness was blind was admissible.

3.5 PRIOR CONSISTENT STATEMENTS/THE RULE AGAINST NARRATIVE

The rule against narrative prohibits statements made by a witness before the trial, which are consistent with his testimony, from being admitted in evidence. Therefore, a witness cannot be asked about such statements, nor can a witness to whom the statement was made be called to testify that it was made. It should be noted that this rule is different from the rule against hearsay. The rule against hearsay prohibits statements made before the trial from being admitted in evidence to prove the truth of their contents where the maker of the statement does not testify. The rule against narrative prevents a witness who does give evidence from being asked by the party who called him about consistent statements made by him before the trial in order to enhance his credibility.

The rationale for this rule is that without it a dishonest litigant could enhance his credibility by repeating his story to a number of people and then have them all testify to show the consistency of his story. This would obviously not be in the interests of justice and would have the added disadvantage of lengthening trials. That said, there are a number of exceptions to this rule where prior consistent statements are admissible: (a) the complaint in sexual offence cases; (b) to rebut an allegation of recent fabrication; (c) evidence of a previous identification; (d) statements admissible under the doctrine of *res gestae*.

3.5.1 The complaint in sexual offence cases

In a sexual offence case, a complaint that is made voluntarily and at the first reasonable opportunity after the commission of the offence is admissible to show the consistency of the complainant. It is only admitted to enhance the credibility of the complainant. It cannot corroborate the complainant's evidence.

The requirement that the complaint be made at the first reasonable opportunity has been examined in a number of cases. In *People (DPP) v Brophy* ([1992] 1 I.L.R.M. 709) O'Flaherty J. in the Court of Criminal Appeal held that "[t]he complaint must have been made as speedily as could reasonably be expected". In this case the prosecution accepted that this test was not satisfied. The complainant had met her mother shortly after the alleged indecent assault and said nothing to her. She only made a complaint later on in the day to her father and some friends.

The test set out in *Brophy* was approved and applied in *People (DPP) v Kiernan* (unreported, March 11, 1994). Here the alleged rape took place on a Friday night upstairs in the appellant's house. After the incident the complainant went downstairs where she met the appellant's girlfriend and told her that the appellant had raped her. The girlfriend did not believe her. She said the complainant must have imagined it. The complainant returned to her parents' home. While there she had an opportunity to make a complaint to her parents and her siblings, but she did not do so. The trial judge and the Court of Criminal Appeal accepted that she was too frightened to tell them. Both courts also accepted that she was justified in not making a complaint until she had an opportunity to make it to her boyfriend. She wanted to make the complaint to her boyfriend because he had an older brother who was a social worker and who the complainant believed she would get good advice from. The complainant met her boyfriend on the Saturday, but she did not say anything to him until she met him again on the Sunday. In those circumstances the court held that if the complaint had been made on the Saturday it would have been admissible, but as it was not made until the Sunday it was inadmissible because it was not made as soon as reasonably possible.

This test was satisfied in *People (DPP) v D.R.* ([1998] 2 I.R. 106). Here the alleged rape took place on a Sunday evening. The complainant was staying overnight at her sister-in-law's house with her husband. Her alleged attacker was her sister-in-law's partner. The complainant had opportunities to complain to her husband and her sister-in-law that night and to her husband while they were on their way home the next morning. The complainant testified that she was frozen by the incident, which had a profound psychological effect on her, which made it difficult to talk about it. She found it hard to complain to her sister-in-law as she was the partner of the man who had carried out the attack. She was also aware that her attacker had a violent temper which he had difficulty controlling and had she complained to her husband in the house she was afraid there would have been a violent confrontation between them. She eventually told her husband about the incident later on the Monday. In those circumstances the trial judge held that the complaint was made as soon as reasonably possible and the Court of Criminal Appeal upheld that finding.

It is equally important that the complaint is made voluntarily or as the court in *Brophy* put it: "not as a result of any inducements or exhortations". In *D.R.*. the appellant tried to argue that as the complaint had been made in answer to a question it should be ruled inadmissible. The court rejected this. The complainant said to her husband that "D is no gentleman" and then he asked her a question. Therefore, the court was satisfied that it was not a question of the husband interrogating the complainant. Instead he "merely assisted her in saying something which she herself wished to say".

The reason why these complaints are admissible is to show consistency. It therefore follows that if the complaint is inconsistent with the account given at trial it will be inadmissible. In *People (DPP) v Gavin* ([2000] 4 I.R. 557) the Court of Criminal Appeal stated: "In this case the complaint was fundamentally inconsistent with the complainant's own evidence at the trial and accordingly, the garda evidence of the complaint should not have been admitted."

3.5.2 To rebut an allegation of recent fabrication

If it is put to a witness during cross-examination that he has recently invented his evidence, statements previously made by the witness may be admitted to show that his testimony is consistent.

3.5.3 Evidence of a previous identification

It is normal for an eyewitness to be asked to identify a suspect at an identification parade before trial. This evidence is admissible at the subsequent trial to show the consistency of the witness.

3.5.4 Statements admissible under the doctrine of *res gestae*

Essentially what we are concerned with here is a statement which is so intertwined with an act that it can be said to be admissible as part of that act. Without the statement the act would not make sense. Therefore, when witnesses are testifying about the act they can refer to the statements made at the time of the act. This doctrine is also an exception to the rule against hearsay and will be considered in more detail in chapter 8.

3.6 REFRESHING MEMORY

Witnesses are allowed to refresh their memory when giving evidence by consulting notes as long as the notes were made contemporaneously with the incident in question. This rule is frequently used, *e.g.* by gardaí witnesses because they are involved in so many cases they might not be able to distinguish between them. The other side may inspect the notes used by the witness to refresh his memory and the witness can be cross-examined on their contents. Even if notes are used the witness must still give oral evidence, he cannot get into the witness box and simply read a prepared statement.

It is also common for a witness to refresh his memory before getting into the witness box by reading a previously made statement. These statements need not have been made contemporaneously with the incident. If a witness does refresh his memory by using notes before testifying then according to *R v Westwell* ([1976] 2 All E.R. 812) the other side must be informed of this fact. Furthermore, the weight to be attached to a witness's testimony could be affected by the fact that they referred to notes.

If a witness uses notes they should not be learned off by heart. The Court of Criminal Appeal made this clear in *People (DPP) v Donnelly* (unreported, February 22, 1999). The court stated:

> "There is clearly a danger that if a witness seeks to learn the contents of his or her statement by heart then when such witness gives evidence in court it may not be about what occurred but about what such witness had said in the statement had occurred. This would clearly be wrong."

3.7 EVIDENCE BY LIVE TELEVISION LINK

Generally witnesses testify in open court. However, in 1989 the Law Reform Commission's *Consultation Paper on Child Sexual Abuse* recognised that the victims of sexual offences find giving evidence in court in front of their attacker extremely traumatic. This report was one of the reasons for the introduction of the Criminal Evidence Act 1992. Part 3 of this Act allows for witnesses in cases where the accused is charged with a sexual or violent offence to give their evidence by a live television link in certain circumstances. Section 13 of the Act provides that a witness may give his evidence by live television link (a) if the person is under 17 years of age, unless the court sees good reason to the contrary; or (b) in any other case, with leave of the court. Section 13(3) provides that while such evidence is being given, neither the judge nor the barristers should wear a wig or gown. Section 14 provides that if it is in the interests of justice the court may require that questions to witnesses under 17 be put to them through an intermediary.

The constitutionality of s.13 of the 1992 Act has been challenged on two occasions. In *White v Ireland* ([1995] 2 I.R. 268) the applicant claimed that an accused had a right to confront his accuser in open court. Kinlen J. rejected this argument. He noted that the jury could view the demeanour of the witness through the television link. He went on to hold that if an accused did have a constitutional right to physically confront a witness that right must yield to the rights of the child.

The Supreme Court approved this judgment in *Donnelly v Ireland* ([1998] 1 I.R. 321). Here the court held that:

> "Fair procedures do not require a case by case determination as to whether a person under the age of 17 years would be traumatised by giving evidence in court in the presence of the accused person and the Oireachtas was entitled to enact legislation permitting the giving of evidence by such persons through a live television link unless the court sees good reason to the contrary."

The television link provisions set out in the 1992 Act have been reproduced in other statutes. Section 39 of the Criminal Justice Act 1999 provides that a witness may give his evidence by live television link where the court is "satisfied that the person is likely to be in fear or subject to intimidation in giving evidence otherwise."

4. CORROBORATION

4.1 INTRODUCTION

This chapter is concerned with unreliable evidence which requires corroboration or a corroboration warning. Therefore, it is important to understand what is meant by corroboration. To corroborate is commonly regarded as meaning to confirm or to support. Traditionally in law, however, its meaning is more complex. This chapter will begin by looking at the legal definition of corroboration. It will then examine the offences that require corroborative evidence to be present before a conviction can be secured. It will be seen that this is a fairly limited category of offences. This is because instead of requiring actual corroboration the common law developed a practice of requiring corroboration warnings to be given in cases relying on certain categories of suspect evidence. This is a warning to a jury of the dangers of convicting someone without the presence of corroborative evidence. The chapter will conclude by analysing when these corroboration warnings are used.

4.2 WHAT EXACTLY IS MEANT BY CORROBORATION?

In *R v Baskerville* ([1916] 2 K.B. 658) Lord Reading C.J. in the Court of Criminal Appeal set out the classic definition of corroboration:

> "We hold that evidence in corroboration must be independent testimony which affects the accused by connecting or tending to connect him with the crime. In other words, it must be evidence which implicates him, that is, which confirms in some material particular not only the evidence that the crime has been committed, but also that the prisoner committed it."

This definition of corroboration has been approved in this jurisdiction. In *People (AG) v Williams* ([1940] I.R. 195) the Supreme Court described corroborative evidence as "independent evidence of material circumstances tending to implicate the accused in the commission of the crime with which he is charged".

The *Baskerville* definition of corroboration is quite narrow. The evidence must be from a totally independent source and it must implicate the accused in the commission of the crime. Both of these requirements will be considered in turn.

4.2.1 Independent evidence

In *People (DPP) v PC* ([2002] 2 I.R. 285) the applicant was convicted of unlawful sexual intercourse. He met the complainant outside her school, and he drove them to his house, where the alleged sex took place in his bedroom. The trial judge gave a corroboration warning to the jury and then told them that the complainant's description of the windows and curtains in the applicant's bedroom was capable of amounting to corroboration of her evidence. The Court of Criminal Appeal quashed his conviction. They held that corroborative evidence must be independent. Self-corroboration is not permissible.

In *R v Redpath* ((1962) 46 Cr. App. R. 319) the court held that the requirement of independence had been satisfied. Here moments after an alleged rape the victim was seen to be in a very distressed condition. It is important to note that the court took into account that the witness was independent and that the complainant was totally unaware that she was being observed.

It is possible for the accused to be the one who provides corroboration, *e.g.* if he makes a confession before the trial begins, if he admits to something during cross-examination or if similar fact evidence (see chapter 6) is admitted. One question, which has not been considered in this jurisdiction, is whether the fact that the accused has lied can provide corroboration of the case against him. In England the Court of Appeal held in *R v Lucas* ([1981] Q.B. 72) that in certain circumstances lies by the accused can amount to corroboration. Four criteria have to be satisfied:

1. The lie must be deliberate;
2. It must relate to a material issue;
3. The motive for the lie must be a realisation of guilt and a fear of the truth;
4. The statement must be clearly shown to be a lie by evidence from an independent witness.

Here the main prosecution witness was an accomplice, not an independent witness, so the accused's lies could not corroborate his testimony. Therefore, his conviction was quashed.

Controversially certain legislation now makes it possible for the silence of an accused to provide corroboration. For example, under ss.18 and 19 of the Criminal Justice Act 1984 adverse inferences may be drawn from a refusal of an accused to explain certain objects in his possession or his presence in a particular place if asked to do so by the gardaí. Although he cannot be convicted solely on the basis of these adverse inferences, they can provide corroboration.

4.2.2 The evidence must implicate the accused in the commission of the crime

In *R v James* ((1971) 55 Cr. App. R. 299) the appellant was convicted of rape. The trial judge's direction gave the jury the impression that they could consider gynaecological evidence that the complainant had had sex around the time of the alleged rape as corroborative of her complaint. The Court of Appeal overturned the accused's conviction because such evidence did not provide corroboration. It did not establish that intercourse was with the accused or that it had been non-consensual. In other words it did not implicate the accused in the commission of a crime.

4.2.3 A change in approach?

Recently it is arguable that there has been a slight move away from the strictness of the *Baskerville* formula. In essence the court in *Baskerville* was trying to ensure that corroborative evidence was reliable. If certain reliable evidence exists which technically falls outside the *Baskerville* definition of corroboration, the courts have shown a willingness to let juries rely on it. For example, if there are several pieces of circumstantial evidence in a case the courts have been prepared to permit their cumulative effect to provide corroboration.

In *People (DPP) v Reid* ([1993] 2 I.R. 186) the appellant was charged with rape (at that time a charge of rape required the complainant's testimony to be corroborated). The victim claimed that the appellant had forced her to come back to his house and raped her in a room with the television on at a high volume to drown out her protests. Keane J. for the Court of Criminal Appeal felt there were "concurring circumstances which [gave] greater probability to the evidence of the prosecutrix". These were, first, medical evidence as to the condition of the complainant's genitals; secondly, the evidence of the complainant's parents and the gardaí as to her distressed condition; and, finally, the evidence of the gardaí that the accused's television was set at a very loud level. It is debatable whether one of these pieces of evidence would have been sufficient on its own.

4.3 WHEN IS CORROBORATION REQUIRED?

Generally it is possible for an accused to be convicted of an offence by the testimony of only one witness. However, there are a few crimes that an accused cannot be convicted of unless the evidence against him is corroborated. At common law corroborative evidence must be present before a jury can convict someone of perjury.

Furthermore, several statutes require corroborative evidence to be present. The Treason Act 1939 requires corroboration before someone can be convicted of treason. Section 105 of the Road Traffic Act 1961 provides that where proof of speed is necessary for the offence, this evidence must be corroborated. Corroboration must also be present for an accused to be convicted of the offence of procuring a woman to be a prostitute under the Criminal Law (Amendment) Act 1885.

4.4 CORROBORATION WARNINGS

Instead of requiring corroboration to be present the common law developed a practice of requiring judges to give a corroboration warning. This warning had to be given when the prosecution's case was based on unreliable evidence. Three categories of witnesses were considered suspect—accomplices, complainants in sexual offence cases and children. In any case which relied exclusively on a witness from one of these groups the trial judge had to caution the jury of the dangers of convicting someone on this uncorroborated evidence. The judge would then tell the jury that they could convict, however, in the absence of corroboration, if they were satisfied of the accused's guilt beyond reasonable doubt. Formerly this warning was mandatory in relation to all three categories, but legislation has been introduced which alters this position. The trial judge now has discretion whether to give the warning or not for complainants in sexual offence cases and for children. However, it remains mandatory in relation to accomplices.

4.4.1 The mandatory corroboration warning for accomplices

4.4.1.1 The rationale for the warning
There are several reasons why the evidence of an accomplice should be treated with suspicion:

(i) An accomplice may attempt to minimise his own role by blaming someone else;

(ii) He may be looking for more favourable treatment from the prosecution and may, on occasion, have been promised immunity or a lighter sentence;

(iii) He may want to shield the real culprit by implicating an innocent party;

(iv) An accomplice is, by definition, a criminal and is therefore arguably an unreliable witness because of his moral culpability;

(v) An accomplice may appear convincing to the jury. He knows all the details of the crime. Therefore, he may be able to concoct a very plausible story, by only changing the details slightly, which would be very difficult to shake in cross-examination.

4.4.1.2 Who is an accomplice?

Because a corroboration warning attaches to accomplice evidence it is very important to establish when someone is an accomplice. The leading case in this area in England is the House of Lords decision in *Davies v DPP* ([1954] A.C. 378). Here the appellant, together with other youths, attacked another gang. During the fight the appellant stabbed and killed one of the other gang. At his trial one of the appellant's associates testified against him. The trial judge did not give the jury a corroboration warning. The appellant claimed that as his friend was an accomplice the jury should have been given a warning. The House of Lords rejected this. Lord Simons L.C. stated:

"persons who are *participes criminis* in respect of the actual crime charged, whether as principals or accessories before or after the fact (in felonies) or persons committing, procuring or aiding and abetting (in the case of misdemeanours). This is surely the natural and primary meaning of the term accomplice."

Therefore, the definition of accomplice must be decided in relation to the specific offence being tried. Here the friend was not an accomplice to the murder as there was no evidence that he intended the attack with the knife. So, if the appellant had been charged with assault then a corroboration warning would have been necessary but no such warning was necessary in relation to the murder charge. It should be noted that the distinction between felonies and misdemeanours has been abolished in this jurisdiction by the Criminal Law Act 1997.

This narrow definition has been widely criticised. In the Australian case of *McNee v Kay* ([1942] V.L.R. 520) Scholl J. pointed out that the temptation to make false accusations was more related to the nature or possible punishment for an offence rather than to its technical identity with that alleged against the accused. Therefore, he suggested an alternative definition. A person "was an accomplice who was chargeable in relation to the same events as those forming the charge against the accused, and who would be, if convicted, liable to such punishment as may tempt him to exaggerate or fabricate evidence as to the guilt of the accused".

This broader approach has found favour in Ireland. In *AG v Linehan* ([1929] I.R. 19) Kennedy C.J. for the Court of Criminal Appeal stated that he did not think that a narrow or precise definition of accomplice should be laid down. But anyone implicated either as principal or as accessory in the crime charged would be an accomplice. Here a woman was charged with the murder of her granddaughter's illegitimate child. The evidence showed that the granddaughter was implicated in the crime, although she had already been acquitted of the offence. The court regarded her as an accomplice so the appellant's conviction was quashed.

In *People (AG) v Carney* ([1955] I.R. 324) the majority of the Supreme Court held that "a very slight degree of complicity, either as principal or accessory, in the crime charged is sufficient to render a person an accomplice for the rule". In *People (DPP) v Diemling* (unreported, May 4, 1992) the Court of Criminal Appeal held that even a slight degree of complicity as an accessory after the fact may be enough to make a witness an accomplice. In *Dental Board v O'Callaghan* ([1969] I.R. 181) an *agent provocateur* was held not to be an accomplice.

4.4.1.3 Accomplice evidence and the witness protection programme

After the murder of the journalist Veronica Guerin a witness protection programme was established by the State. This development led to a difficulty for the courts. How should they treat the evidence of an accomplice who had benefited significantly under this programme?

One of first cases to deal with this issue was *People (DPP) v Ward* (unreported, Court of Criminal Appeal, March 22, 2002). Here the appellant was convicted of murder in the Special Criminal Court largely on the uncorroborated testimony of an accomplice, Charles Bowden. For testifying Bowden received a monetary payment, immunity from prosecution and he and his family were given new identities. The defence had argued that because of this Bowden should be regarded as a "supergrass" and, therefore, his evidence should be treated with greater scepticism than an ordinary accomplice. The Special Criminal Court accepted that Bowden "would lie without hesitation and regardless of the consequences for others if he perceived it to be in his own interest to do so". Notwithstanding this they held that he should be treated as an ordinary accomplice. Furthermore, while they accepted that it was unsafe to convict on the uncorroborated evidence of an accomplice, they did so here as they felt his evidence was truthful.

The Court of Criminal Appeal quashed the appellant's conviction. Murphy J., giving judgment for the court, did not dwell on whether Bowden fell within the category of a "supergrass". Instead he focused on the facts that he was an "inveterate liar", whose testimony was shown to be inaccurate under cross-examination and who had received considerable benefits for his family under the witness protection programme. He held:

> "Whether or not Charles Bowden fell within the category compromised in the slang expression 'supergrass', clearly his lack of general credibility and his position as a criminal negotiating with the authorities to secure advantages for himself at the expense of his former friends and criminal associates did require that his evidence should be considered with the utmost care."

In *People (DPP) v Gilligan* (unreported, Court of Criminal Appeal, August 8, 2003) the evidence of accomplices, who had also obtained benefits under the witness protection programme, helped secure the appellant's conviction. Here the Court of Criminal Appeal upheld the appellant's conviction. However, the Court certified two questions of public importance for consideration by the Supreme Court. One of these was whether corroboration (as distinct from a mere corroboration warning) is required in respect of the testimony of accomplice witnesses who have participated in the State witness protection programme. The Supreme Court's judgment on this point has yet to be delivered. It will undoubtedly have a significant impact on this area of law.

4.4.1.4 *Who decides whether someone is an accomplice, the judge or the jury?*

According to the House of Lords in *Davies v DPP* ([1954] A.C. 378) three possible situations can be distinguished:

(i)   Sometimes it is clear that a witness is an accomplice—here the trial judge must give a corroboration warning;

(ii)   On other occasions it is equally obvious that a witness is not an accomplice—here no corroboration warning should be given;

(iii)   Finally, there could be a borderline case where there is evidence from which a reasonable jury could find that the witness is an accomplice. Here the trial judge should leave it to the jury to decide for themselves whether or not the witness is an accomplice. (Therefore, the judge will give a conditional corroboration warning—one that is conditional on the jury accepting that the witness is an accomplice).

In Ireland the position in relation to this last category has caused some controversy. In *People (AG) v Carney* the two defendants were convicted of receiving stolen goods, mainly on the evidence of a witness who the Supreme Court said was clearly an accomplice. The trial judge left it to the jury to decide if the witness was an accomplice. The Court of Criminal Appeal approved this decision. They held that even where the evidence points strongly to the witness being an accomplice, it is up to the jury to resolve that question. However, the majority of the Supreme Court rejected this approach. They held that where it is clear on the evidence that the witness is an accomplice, this issue should not be left to the jury and accordingly the warning given should have been absolute. Dixon J. dissented; he felt that the issue should have been left to the jury. Despite the strong evidence, he felt that if it had been at all possible for the jury to take the view that the witness was not an accomplice, then this issue should have been left to them.

In *DPP v Diemling* the trial judge decided that the witness was not an accomplice and so did not leave the matter to the jury. The Court of Criminal Appeal found that the witness may have been an accessory after the fact and so was capable of being considered an accomplice. This issue was a matter of fact for the jury to decide and, therefore, the trial judge should have given them a conditional warning.

4.4.2 Discretionary corroboration warnings

Two categories of evidence will be considered under this heading: the evidence of complainants in sexual offence cases and the evidence of children.

4.4.2.1 Complainants in sexual offence cases

Historically, the evidence of complainants in sexual offence cases was treated with suspicion. Therefore, it became common for judges to give such evidence a corroboration warning. According to the Court of Criminal Appeal in *People (AG) v Cradden* ([1955] I.R. 130) this practice had the force of a rule of law. If a warning was not given, a conviction would be overturned. The rationale for this rule was the view that such complaints were easily made and hard to disprove. So for example in *People (AG) v Williams* ([1940] I.R. 195), the Supreme Court noted: "In cases of rape the prosecutrix is not *prima facie* a discredited witness, as is an accomplice, nevertheless it has been recognised ... that the jury should consider her evidence with particular care and should look for some confirmation of it". Obviously this rationale, particularly the view that complaints of this nature are easily made, has no foundation and the rule has now rightly been abolished.

Section 7 of the Criminal Law (Rape) (Amendment) Act 1990 provides that in a sexual offence case the trial judge now has a discretion as to whether to give such a warning or not. The section also states that if a judge decides to give the warning, it is not necessary for him to use any particular form of words.

After the introduction of the legislation the question remained as to how judges would exercise their discretion, particularly as the old practice was one developed by the judiciary in the first place. There was concern that judges would simply exercise their discretion in favour of giving a warning in every case.

This concern initially appeared justified. For example, in *People (DPP) v Molloy* (unreported, July 28, 1995) Flood J. on behalf of the Court of Criminal Appeal stated:

> "this Court is of the view that where the charge is essentially supported by the evidence of the Complainant alone without collateral forensic evidence or any other form of corroboration, it is a prudent practice for the trial Judge to warn the jury that unless they are very satisfied with the testimony of the Complainant that they should be careful not to convict in the absence of corroborative evidence".

However, a new approach by the judiciary is now evident. In *People (DPP) v JEM* ([2001] 4 I.R. 385) the applicant was appealing against his conviction for sexual assault mainly on the ground that the trial judge had failed to give the jury a corroboration warning. Denham J. on behalf of the Court of Criminal Appeal made clear that the warning was no longer mandatory. She approved the decision of the English Court of Appeal in *R v Makanjuola* ([1995] 1 W.L.R. 1348) which was based on a similarly worded UK statute. She endorsed the following principles laid down in that case:

> "1) Section 32(1) abrogates the requirement to give a corroboration direction in respect of an alleged accomplice or a complainant of a sexual offence simply because a witness falls into one of these categories. [Section 32(1) is the applicable provision in the UK where accomplice evidence also only attracts a discretionary warning].
>
> 2) It is a matter for the judge's discretion what, if any, warning he considers appropriate in respect of such a witness, as indeed in respect of any other witness in whatever type of case. Whether he chooses to give a warning and in what terms will depend on the circumstances of the case, the issues raised and the content and quality of the witness's evidence.
>
> 3) In some cases, it may be appropriate for the judge to warn the jury to exercise caution before acting upon the unsupported evidence of a witness. This will not be so simply because the witness is the complainant

of a sexual offence nor will it necessarily be so because a witness is alleged to be an accomplice. There will need to be an evidential basis for suggesting that the evidence of the witness may be unreliable. An evidential basis does not include mere suggestions by cross-examining counsel.

4) If any question arises as to whether the judge should give a special warning in respect of a witness, it is desirable that the question be resolved by discussion with counsel in the absence of the jury before final speeches.

5) Where the judge does decide to give some warning in respect of a witness, it would be appropriate to do so as part of the judge's review of the evidence and his comments as to how the jury should evaluate it rather than as a set-piece of legal direction.

6) Where some warning is required, it would be for the judge to decide the strength and terms of the warning. It does not have to be invested with the whole florid regime of the old corroboration rules.

7) Attempts to re-impose the straightjacket of the old corroboration rules are strongly to be deprecated.

8) Finally, this court will be disinclined to interfere with a trial judge's exercise of his discretion save in a case where that exercise is unreasonable."

The view taken by Denham J. was approved in *People (DPP) v Wallace* (unreported, April 30 2001). Here Keane J. stated that the abolition of the mandatory corroboration warning by the legislature should not be circumvented by trial judges simply adopting the cautious approach of giving the warning in every case where there is no corroboration. Therefore, it is clear that a trial judge should have an evidential basis for giving the warning rather than simply basing it on the fact that the complainant was the victim of a sexual offence.

An example of a case where there was such an evidential basis is the Court of Criminal Appeal decision in *People (DPP) v PJ* ([2003] 3 I.R. 550). Here McGuinness J. held that there were several difficulties with the prosecution's case that justified the trial judge's decision to give the warning. They were firstly that the complainant's evidence contained a number of inconsistencies and was vague in some respects, particularly about dates. Secondly, the offences were alleged to have taken place in a house with many inhabitants, none of whom gave any evidence of witnessing the offences. Finally, there was no evidence given as to physical injuries which might have been suffered as a result of repeated rape.

4.4.2.2 Children's evidence

Until recently the sworn evidence of a child attracted a mandatory corroboration warning. Additionally, the Children Act 1908 provided that the unsworn evidence of a child had to be corroborated before it could lead to an accused's conviction. There were several reasons why the evidence of children was treated with such mistrust. There was a fear that a child may not fully appreciate the importance of telling the truth when testifying; their recollection of events may be less accurate than that of an adult; their testimony could be influenced by an adult; and it was not possible to cross-examine a child as forcefully as one would an adult.

However, in modern times some of these justifications have been questioned. Furthermore, as society became aware of the prevalence of child sexual abuse there was a fear that these old rules would make prosecutions near impossible. In its report on Child Sexual Abuse in 1990 the Law Reform Commission recommended that the rules be abolished.

This report led to the introduction of the Criminal Evidence Act 1992. Section 28(1) of this Act abolishes the absolute requirement for corroboration in respect of the unsworn evidence of children. Section 28 also provides that any requirement that the jury be given a compulsory corroboration warning by the judge about convicting on the evidence of a child is also abolished. The trial judge now has discretion to decide whether a particular child's evidence requires a corroboration warning. Finally, unsworn evidence received by virtue of s.28 may corroborate evidence given by another person.

5. IDENTIFICATION EVIDENCE

5.1 INTRODUCTION

Like the categories of evidence discussed in the previous chapter, identification evidence is also considered unreliable. This is because mistaken identifications have led to innocent people being convicted in the past. Indeed in the UK the Devlin Report on Evidence of Identification in 1972 stated that "cases of mistaken identification constituted by far the greatest cause of actual or possible wrong convictions".

5.2 RATIONALE

There are a number of reasons for this:

1. The conditions may have been poor when the identification was made, *e.g.* it may have been dark; the weather may have been bad; or the witness may have been a considerable distance away.
2. The witness may have bad eyesight, they may have only seen the person for a brief moment, they may have been in a state of shock, or they may have had no special reason to remember the person.
3. The usual method of discovering errors or inconsistencies in testimony, cross-examination, is ineffective here; the witness identifies the person and that is it. It is extremely difficult for the defence to undermine such evidence. In fact, if the defence attempt to do so it could easily backfire as the witness may simply reinforce their previous testimony.

5.3 THE IDENTIFICATION WARNING

For these reasons judges must now give a special warning to juries in any case that depends largely on visual identification evidence. The Supreme Court established this in *People (AG) v Casey (No.2)* ([1963] I.R. 33). The appellant was convicted of offences contrary to the Offences Against the Person Act 1861. His conviction was based substantially on his identification by two witnesses who were not known to him previously. One was an 11-year-old boy who had been involved in the incident and the other an adult who had given chase to him after the event and caught a momentary glimpse of him in the headlamps of his car. The Court of Criminal Appeal upheld his conviction; however, on a point of law of public importance, the case went to the Supreme Court.

The Supreme Court ordered a retrial. Giving judgment for the Supreme Court, Kingsmill Moore J. concluded that juries were not sufficiently aware of the dangers involved in identification evidence or of the number of cases where identifications had proved to be incorrect and that there was a danger that a jury would attach too much probative effect to a positive identification. Therefore, he held that there should be a warning given, in all cases, wholly or substantially dependent on visual identification evidence.

He then formulated the direction that a trial judge should give to a jury in such cases. He stated that the jury should be warned that there have been a number of cases where honest witnesses with ample time to observe a person and who made positive identifications were subsequently shown to be incorrect and they should, therefore, be cautious about accepting such evidence as correct. However, if after careful consideration of such evidence, together with all the other evidence, they are satisfied beyond reasonable doubt that the identification is correct, they may convict.

He also said that the warning should not be a stereotyped formula, rather it should vary according to the facts of the case, so where the witness had not had a prior relationship with the defendant, or where the witness had only a brief time to observe the wrong-doer, the warning should be stronger. He mentioned, however, that there must be a minimum warning which must be given in any case which depends on visual identification. He also added that the warning should not be confined to cases where the identification is that of only one witness.

In the United Kingdom, the leading case in this area is the decision of the Court of Appeal in *R v Turnbull* ([1977] 1 Q.B. 224). This case, which came after the *Casey* decision, laid down several guidelines for visual identification evidence:

1. The court stated that whenever a case depends wholly or substantially on the identification of the accused, which the defence claims is mistaken, the judge should warn the jury of a special need for caution before convicting the accused.

2. He should also tell them why there is a need for such a warning.
3. The judge should direct the jury to examine closely the circumstances of the identification, *e.g.* how long was the accused observed? At what distance?
4. They should be reminded of any specific weaknesses in the identification.
5. If the quality of the identification evidence is good and the jury are warned to be cautious, then they can be left to assess the value of the identifying evidence.
6. When the quality of the identifying evidence is poor (*e.g.* only a fleeting glance) the judge should withdraw the case from the jury and direct an acquittal unless there is other evidence, which goes to support the correctness of the identification.

The court stated that a failure to follow these guidelines is likely to result in a conviction being quashed. These guidelines have been approved in Ireland in several cases, *e.g. People (DPP) v Stafford* ([1983] I.R. 165).

It is worth noting that the Supreme Court in *Casey* and the Court of Appeal in *Turnbull* used the phrase "supporting evidence" rather than corroboration. Essentially the courts were anxious to ensure there was a safeguard against exclusive reliance on unreliable identification evidence. What they did not want to do, however, was to burden this area of law with a requirement of corroboration. This was because, as was seen in the last chapter, the *Baskerville* definition of corroboration is very narrow. Supporting evidence is a far broader concept. In *Turnbull* the court gave the following illustrative example of their reasoning. A witness sees the accused snatch a woman's handbag. He gets only a fleeting glance of the thief as he runs off but he does see him entering a nearby house. Later, he picks out the accused at an identity parade. If there were no more evidence than this, the poor quality of the identification would require the judge to withdraw the case from the jury. But this would not be so if there were evidence that the house into which the accused was alleged to have run was his father's. However, in a strict legal sense, it could not be corroborative evidence, as a witness cannot corroborate his or her own testimony.

5.3.1 Recognition evidence

It has been accepted in a number of cases in this jurisdiction that the *Casey* warning should be given in cases of recognition evidence. In *People (DPP) v Stafford* ([1983] I.R. 165) the two prosecution witnesses who identified the accused knew him for a number of years before the incident. On that basis the trial judge distinguished this case from *Casey*. He did not give the jury the standard warning about accepting identification evidence. Instead he said that this case was about the veracity of the witnesses, not identification. The Court of Criminal Appeal ordered a re-trial. They held that even where the witnesses recognise the accused a *Casey* warning should still be given to the jury.

The Court of Criminal Appeal has recently confirmed this position in *People (DPP) v Smith* ([1999] 2 I.L.R.M. 161). Here it was held that although there is a distinction between recognition evidence and mere visual identification, which makes the former generally more reliable, this would not justify abandoning the *Casey* rule.

5.4 THE MEANS OF IDENTIFICATION

A witness is not normally permitted to identify an accused for the first time in court (this is known as dock identification). In *People (DPP) v Cooney* ([1998] 1 I.L.R.M. 321) the Supreme Court made clear that this is very prejudicial to the accused. This is because with the trial already under way a witness may feel pressurised into identifying the accused. Therefore, it should only be permitted in exceptional circumstances.

Instead what should happen is that the accused is identified before the trial commences. Initially the courts were ambivalent as to how this identification should occur. So in *People (AG) v Martin* ([1956] I.R. 22) the Supreme Court held that there was no rule of law or practice that required identification to be proved by way of an identification parade and that each case must be considered on its own facts. Similarly in *People (AG) v Fagan* (unreported, May 13, 1974) the Court of Criminal Appeal held that "other types of identification may in certain circumstances be fairer and more dependable than a formal identification parade which ... may be a less than satisfactory means of achieving a reliable identification".

However, in more recent times it has been accepted that the holding of a formal identification parade is best practice. In *People (DPP) v Duff* ([1995] 3 I.R. 296) the Court of Criminal Appeal stated:

> "the proper, regular and optimum method of holding an identification for a witness who believes he or she can visually identify an accused person in a criminal case is an identification parade. Any other method of visual identification where it is a real issue in the case is necessarily a second-best".

After the parade the witness should then make a further identification in open court confirming the previous identification.

Nowadays there may be difficulties in securing a conviction in any case in which identification is an issue if a formal identification parade does not take place and at the very least the trial judge would be expected to give a stronger *Casey* warning.

In *People (DPP) v O'Reilly* ([1990] 2 I.R. 415) the applicant was convicted of larceny and appealed. The main prosecution witness was the victim, an 81-year-old woman. A man offering to do work for her had approached her in her garden. He asked for a drink of water and she gave it to him. Later she discovered some money was missing. About two months later she was taken by the gardaí to a local courthouse. As a group of people went in she thought she recognised one of them but she was uncertain, as she did not get a good look at him. When the people emerged from the courthouse she said, "that's him, the fellow with the ugly face". The defence argued that the evidence of identification should not have been admitted in the absence of a satisfactory explanation as to why a formal identification parade was not held. In quashing the applicant's conviction O'Flaherty J. on behalf of the Court of Criminal Appeal held that an identification parade should have been held. The court went on to state that the holding of an identification parade is an important filter for the prosecution and the defence. If a suspect is not picked out at a parade then the prosecution may go no further. Conversely, if he is picked out he may decide to plead guilty.

The courts have recognised that it will not always be possible or practical to hold a formal identification parade. For example, in *O'Reilly* the court suggested that if the accused was of singular appearance it might be impossible to get sufficient people to conduct a fair parade. Similarly, the court accepted that if the witness knows the accused then it would be senseless to hold a formal identification parade. Furthermore, the court pointed out that, if a suspect refuses to take part in a formal identification parade, he may have to live with the consequences.

The case of *People (DPP) v Rapple* ([1999] 1 I.L.R.M. 113) is an example of a case where the accused refused to take part in a formal identification parade. He was subsequently identified from the passenger seat of a car as he walked down a road. It was held that the gardaí were entitled to hold an informal identification parade where the option of a formal identification parade was refused. However, the particular informal identification procedure must be fair to the accused. This would presumably exclude identifications made, *e.g.* outside a courthouse, which is clearly prejudicial.

The prosecution have on occasion attempted to use other excuses to justify the failure to hold an identification parade. In *Fagan* the court rejected the excuse put forward that as the accused was not living at home he was not readily available for a parade. The court also rejected the purported justification put forward in *O'Reilly*. Here one of the garda witnesses claimed that a formal identification parade was not held because it was more beneficial to the defendant not to hold one and that an informal identification was fairer. While accepting that it was right that those involved in prosecution should be scrupulous in looking to the rights of the accused, O'Flaherty J. nonetheless felt that the decision as to what is most beneficial for an accused in the preparation and conduct of his defence, must be primarily a matter for the accused and his legal advisers.

5.5 THE CHARACTERISTICS OF THE WITNESS

It is clear that the characteristics or attributes of the witness are something that the courts take into account. In *O'Reilly* the trial judge gave the jury a warning in accordance with *Casey*. However, the Court of Criminal Appeal agreed with the appellant's submissions that the warning should have been much stronger because of the infirmities of the injured party. She was 81, she was in a state of shock and she was in a good deal of pain from an arthritic condition. Conversely in *People (DPP) v O'Callaghan* (unreported, July 30, 1990), the fact that the witness was a security guard who was experienced in observation helped the prosecution case.

5.6 THE USE OF PHOTOGRAPHS

Obviously it is important for the gardaí to be able to use photos when investigating crimes. However, their use raises a number of difficulties for an accused.

1. Once a witness says he recognises someone from a photo it will be difficult for him to separate in his mind the image of the person he initially saw from the image in the photo.
2. An uncertain witness may be reassured by the fact that as the gardaí have this photo on file the person must have come to their attention previously.
3. The fact that the witness has been shown a photo of the accused undermines the value of the identification. However, the defence face a dilemma in deciding whether to raise this issue. If they raise it the jury will then know that the accused has come to the gardaí's attention previously.

The courts have considered the use of photos by the gardaí in a number of cases.

In *People (DPP) v Rapple* the Court of Criminal Appeal distinguished between two situations, one where photos could be used and one where they should not be. The court accepted that it was a proper investigative procedure for the gardaí to take a description of the offender from a witness and then show them photos of people matching that description. However, what the gardaí should not do is show a witness a photo just to establish whether they would make a positive identification of someone they already suspect at a later formal identification parade.

In *O'Reilly* the court expressed concern at the fact that photographs of the accused were shown to the witness prior to her going to identify the accused. This further substantiated the court's fears that this was an identification obtained in unusual and doubtful circumstances, which rendered the conviction unsafe.

5.7 THE USE OF VIDEOTAPE FOOTAGE

Videotape footage has the advantage over photos in that it can be played for the jury. In *R v Dodson* ([1984] 1 W.L.R. 971) the English Court of Appeal held that if a video is sufficiently clear a jury could be permitted to look at it and compare the person recorded with the accused. However, to convict they must be satisfied beyond reasonable doubt that the accused is the person on the video. The Court of Criminal Appeal approved this judgment in *People (DPP) v Maguire* ([1995] 2 I.R. 286).

Video evidence was also used in *People (DPP) v O'Callaghan* (unreported, July 30, 1990). Here one of the main prosecution witnesses was a security guard who caught a brief look at the robber before he was told to lie on the floor. The robber was in disguise, he was wearing a wig, a hat, a false nose and a moustache. The incident was caught on camera and having watched the tape twice it struck the witness that the robber was one of two men who had behaved suspiciously two days previously. After watching the earlier video he was satisfied that he could identify the accused. The jury saw both videos. The trial judge had refused an application to withdraw the case from the jury. The Court of Criminal Appeal upheld that decision, noting that the witness was a security guard experienced in observation.

5.7.1 Videotape footage and the prosecution's duty to seek out and preserve evidence

A number of recent cases involving videotape evidence have established that the gardaí have a duty to seek out and preserve evidence. This duty will be considered here although it is clear that it applies to more than just identification evidence. In *Braddish v DPP* ([2002] 1 I.L.R.M. 151) a shop was robbed in July 1997. The shop was protected by video surveillance and the gardaí, having viewed the tape, believed it to show the robbery in progress. In October 1997 the appellant was arrested on foot of the video evidence and while being detained allegedly made a confession. However, he was not charged until July 1998. At his first appearance in the District Court his solicitor asked for a copy of the tape. He made a written request for the tape in December 1998. In January 1999 the solicitor was informed that the tape was not available, as it had been returned to the shop after the appellant had confessed. The appellant then applied to have his prosecution restrained. He claimed he could not get a fair trial because he was not furnished with the tape. In the High Court O'Caoimh J. refused his application as the prosecution were relying on his confession rather than the videotape. However, the Supreme Court overturned this decision. Hardiman J. noted that the alleged confession was disputed and further that a confession should be corroborated. He held that:

> "It is the duty of the Gardaí, arising from their unique in-
> vestigative role, to seek out and preserve all evidence hav-
> ing a bearing or potential bearing on the issue of guilt or
> innocence. This is so whether the prosecution proposes to
> rely on the evidence or not, and regardless of whether it
> assists the case the prosecution is advancing or not."

The Supreme Court considered this issue again in *Dunne v DPP* ([2002] 2 I.L.R.M. 241). Once again the appellant was charged with the robbery of a petrol station. On previous occasions relevant videotapes from the petrol station had been acquired by the gardaí. However, in this case the gardaí stated that they had never obtained the videotape. Hardiman J. gave the majority judgment. He noted that it would be difficult to think of evidence more directly relevant than a videotape showing the offence in progress. He held that there was a duty on the prosecution "to take reasonable steps to seek out material evidence". Fennelly J. dissented; he felt that this case could be distinguished from *Braddish* as it was never shown that the tape was in the gardaí's possession.

6. LEADING EVIDENCE OF AN ACCUSED'S PREVIOUS CONVICTIONS (SIMILAR FACT EVIDENCE)

6.1 INTRODUCTION

It is common for evidence textbooks to contain a chapter entitled "Similar Fact Evidence"; however, this title may initially cause confusion. What such chapters in fact deal with is a general rule of evidence, which provides that the prosecution are not permitted to lead evidence of an accused's bad character or previous criminal record. The phrase "similar fact evidence" was used as a convenient catch-all phrase to describe the exceptions to the rule. The reason why this phrase was chosen was that initially for evidence of an accused's previous convictions to be admissible in a subsequent trial, the facts of the two incidents had to be similar. The test for admissibility is now somewhat different, but the original name has remained. Currently bad character evidence is only admissible if its probative effect outweighs its prejudicial value. This chapter will examine how this test emerged.

6.2 RATIONALE

The rationale for this exclusionary rule is that bad character evidence is very prejudicial. For example, the jury may consider that as the accused is of bad character he is more likely to be guilty, or they may consider that the accused deserves to be punished for his previous crimes even though they are not satisfied of his present guilt beyond reasonable doubt. On the other hand, in some situations such evidence may be very probative indeed, *e.g.* surely a jury are entitled to know if an accused has used a particular *modus operandi* in the past. Therefore, the law in this area must strike a balance between these two competing arguments. The current test of admissibility attempts to do this.

6.3 THE DEVELOPMENT OF THE RULE

The starting point for this analysis is the decision of the Privy Council in *Makin v AG for New South Wales* ([1894] A.C. 57). Here the two accused were husband and wife. They were charged with the murder of a baby they had adopted. The baby's bones were discovered buried in the garden of a house the couple used to live in.

After they were charged the police dug up three other gardens of houses occupied at different times by the accused. They found the bodies of 13 other babies. At their trial for the murder of the first baby the prosecution sought to introduce this fact into evidence. The defence counsel objected, claiming that evidence of previous misconduct was inadmissible. In a now celebrated passage, Lord Herschell stated:

> "It is undoubtedly not competent for the prosecution to adduce evidence tending to show that the accused has been guilty of criminal acts other than those covered by the indictment, for the purpose of leading to the conclusion that the accused is a person likely from his criminal conduct or character to have committed the offence for which he is tried. On the other hand, the mere fact that the evidence adduced tends to shew [sic] the commission of other crimes does not render it inadmissible if it be relevant to an issue before the jury, and it may be so relevant if it bears upon the question whether the acts alleged to constitute the crime charged in the indictment were designed or accidental, or to rebut a defence which would otherwise be open to the accused".

Applying this test to the facts of the case it was held that the evidence was admissible in order to rebut the defence of inevitable accident.

The test set out in *Makin* was followed in Ireland. In *People (AG) v Kirwan* ([1943] I.R. 279) the accused was charged with the murder of his brother. The prosecution wanted to introduce evidence of the fact that the accused had recently spent time in prison. They had two reasons for this. First, the deceased's body had been expertly dismembered and the medical evidence was that whoever did this had some expertise, *e.g.* a vet or a butcher. The accused had learnt how to be a butcher while in prison and had dismembered carcasses of pigs there in a similar fashion. Secondly, the deceased had £200 in his house when he was killed. The accused had been spending freely since his brother's disappearance and was arrested with £80 on him. The fact that he had been in prison for most of the last four years suggested that he would not have had any savings of his own. This evidence was allowed to go to the jury under the *Makin* test.

In *Makin* Lord Herschell warned that the principles he was setting out would be difficult to apply in practice. This turned out to be correct. Lord Herschell had given two examples of when evidence might be admissible to show whether acts were designed or accidental or to rebut a defence. Although only given as examples because of the difficulties with applying the test, the courts began to regard them as categories which evidence had to fall into to be admissible. This development was inappropriate as there are other categories of evidence which should be admissible.

Another issue also became apparent after *Makin*. Lord Herschell in his judgment reviewed previous case law. In this review he highlighted the fact that for misconduct evidence to be admissible it had to be exceptional and he suggested that one way for it to be exceptional was if it showed a systematic course of conduct by the accused. In subsequent cases this suggestion developed into a requirement that the previous misconduct had to be strikingly similar to the facts in the case being considered. This explains the development of the phrase "similar fact evidence".

The House of Lords considered both of these issues in *Boardman v DPP* ([1974] 3 All E.R. 887). The appellant was the headmaster of a boarding school for boys. He was charged on three counts; the House of Lords, however, was only concerned with two, the buggery of one boy and incitement to commit buggery with another. The trial judge had, in his summing-up, told the jury that because of some unusual features in the case it was open to them to find that the story of one boy corroborated that of the other boy. The unusual features were that both boys had been woken up in the early hours of the morning in their dorm and spoken to in a low voice so as not to wake the other boys, and had been taken to Boardman's sitting room, where they were asked to take the active part, while the appellant took the passive part, in acts of buggery. It was held by the House of Lords that the evidence of each boy in relation to the offence concerning him was admissible in deciding whether Boardman had committed the offence in relation to the other boy. This was the unanimous decision of the court, however, the court gave five separate judgments and unfortunately they are not all completely consistent with one another as to what the correct test for the admissibility of misconduct evidence is.

Having said that, it is clear that in determining admissibility all five lords placed emphasis on the striking similarities between the evidence given by the two complainants. This can be seen from a passage by Lord Wilberforce where it is clear that a striking similarity was required for the evidence to be admissible:

"The basic principle must be that the admission of similar fact evidence…is exceptional and requires a strong degree of probative force. This probative force is derived, if at all, from the circumstance that the facts testified to by the several witnesses bear to each other such a striking similarity that they must, when judged by experience and common sense, either all be true, or have arisen from a cause common to the witnesses or from pure coincidence."

After *Boardman* the courts focused on whether there were striking similarities between the incidents. This can be clearly seen from the judgment in *R v Mansfield* ([1978] 1 All E.R. 134). Here the accused was charged with three counts of arson in relation to three fires that occurred in hotels owned by his employer. There were several similarities between the incidents which together were sufficiently striking for the trial judge to permit the evidence to go to the jury. In each case the arsonist poured a flammable material onto the hotel carpet and ignited it. The accused was seen near each of the fires behaving suspiciously. Furthermore, two of the fires had been started in areas of the hotels that only the staff had access to. This suggested that an employee was responsible. Only two employees had worked in all three hotels and it was clear that the other employee was not involved. The Court of Appeal upheld the trial judge's view that all this evidence combined was strikingly similar.

However, there were a number of problems with this requirement of striking similarity. The rule was very time-consuming as it basically required a trial judge to examine much of the evidence in a particular case to establish if it could be described as strikingly similar to the facts of a previous incident. Furthermore, it was not clear what exactly striking meant. In fact in *Boardman* itself Lord Wilberforce acknowledged that what is striking in one age is normal in another. Therefore, trial judges had to decide for themselves when the requirement was satisfied. This could lead to inconsistencies in borderline cases.

For example, the Court of Appeal came to a different conclusion in two cases with similar facts. In *R v Novac* ((1977) 65 Cr. App. R. 107 (C.A.)) and *R v Johannsen* ((1977) 65 Cr. App. Rep. 101) the two accused were charged with several counts of buggery. They both allegedly picked up all their victims at amusement arcades and brought them back to their houses. In *Novac*, the Court of Appeal found that these facts were not strikingly similar so the evidence of one boy was not admissible in relation to the charges concerning the other boys. However, in *Johannsen*, the Court of Appeal found that this evidence was strikingly similar and was therefore admissible.

These difficulties led the Court of Appeal in *DPP v P* ([1991] 2 A.C. 447) to suggest that it was time for the House of Lords to re-examine their judgment in *Boardman*. Here the accused was convicted of the rape and incest of his two daughters. At the beginning of the case the defence applied to have the case against each daughter tried separately. This application was refused by the trial judge on the basis that the evidence of each girl was admissible in the case relating to the other, as there were striking similarities between their accounts. Both daughters gave evidence of the prolonged nature of the abuse, the use of force by the accused, the control he had over them and the fact that he had paid for abortions for both of them. The accused was convicted. However, his appeal to the Court of Appeal was successful. The problem for the court was that they felt his behaviour could not be said to be strikingly similar. It was "stock in trade" behaviour that was seen in most child abuse cases. Therefore, they concluded that as the evidence was not strikingly similar it was inadmissible. They certified a point of law of exceptional public importance and the issue went to the House of Lords. The House of Lords reinterpreted *Boardman*. They held that:

> "the essential feature of evidence which is to be admitted is that its probative force in support of the allegation that an accused committed a crime is sufficiently great to make it just to admit the evidence, notwithstanding that it is prejudicial to the accused in tending to show that he was guilty of another crime. Such probative force may be derived from striking similarities in the evidence…But restricting the circumstances in which there is sufficient probative force to overcome prejudice of evidence relating to another crime to cases in which there is some striking similarity between them is to restrict the operation of the principle in a way which gives too much effect to a particular manner of stating it, and is not justified in principle."

This test has been approved in this jurisdiction. In *B v DPP* ([1997] 3 I.R. 140) the applicant was charged in 1993 with numerous counts of indecent assault and rape of his three daughters between 1962 and 1974. He applied for an order prohibiting the trial because of the prejudice he would suffer in defending himself due to the delay between the date he was charged and the date of the alleged incidents. He also claimed he would suffer prejudice because of the large number of offences alleged on the indictment. In dealing with this latter issue Budd J. had to consider whether the evidence of one daughter was admissible in relation to the charges concerning the other daughters. He accepted that the evidence of the daughters was strikingly similar. All had been abused from a very young age in the absence of their mother, all had been subjected to acts of sexual self-gratification on the part of the father and, in all cases, these acts had been accompanied by threats of violence in the event of resistance or disclosure. However, he then acknowledged that *DPP v P* had changed the test in England. He stated: "more recently stress has been laid on the positive probative value of the evidence rather than the use of striking similarity as the test for the admissibility in cases." He then quoted at length from the House of Lords judgment in *DPP v P* and concluded that for the evidence to be admissible it had to have "a sufficient degree of probative force" to overcome its prejudicial effect.

The leading Irish case on this issue is the judgment of the Court of Criminal Appeal in *People (DPP) v BK* ([2000] 2 I.R. 199). Here the applicant worked in a residential home for children. He was charged with 10 counts of sexual offences against various boys in the home. At the beginning of the trial several counts were withdrawn by the prosecution so they only proceeded with four counts. In counts one and two he was charged with indecent assault and buggery against one boy. In counts eight and nine he was charged with attempted buggery of two other boys. At the end of the trial the jury could not agree on counts one and two but they convicted him on counts eight and nine. The applicant sought leave to appeal on the basis that each of the counts, in so far as they related to a different boy, should have been tried separately. The prosecution claimed that there was a sufficient similarity between the offences for them to be tried together. Barron J. for the Court of Criminal Appeal held that the test as to whether the counts should be heard together was whether the evidence of each boy was admissible on the counts relating to the other boys. It therefore had to decide whether this evidence was admissible. Barron J. held:

"For such evidence to be so admissible, it would be necessary for the probative value of such evidence to outweigh its prejudicial effect. In practice, this test is applied where there is a similarity between the facts relating to several counts."

He then went through the previous cases on this issue, including *Makin*, *Boardman*, *DPP v P* and *B v DPP*. From these judgments Barron J. extracted the following principles:

"1)   The rules of evidence should not be allowed to offend the common sense.
2)   So, where the probative value of evidence outweighs the prejudicial effect, it may be admitted.
3)   The categories of cases in which the evidence can be so admitted, is not closed.
4)   Such evidence is admitted in two main types of cases:

(a)   to establish that the same person committed each offence because of the particular feature common to each; or
(b)   where the charges are against one person only, to establish that offences were committed.

In the latter case the evidence is admissible because:

(a)   there is the inherent improbability of several persons making up exactly similar stories;
(b)   it shows a practice, which would rebut an accident, innocent explanation or denial."

Applying these principles the court held that counts one and two should not have been joined with counts eight and nine as the evidence went no further than saying that because the applicant was charged with offences against one boy, he was more likely to have committed the offences alleged against the other boys. It accepted that all the alleged offences were against boys in the applicant's care in the same residential home. However, counts one and two were alleged to have been committed in a dormitory at night and counts eight and nine were alleged to have been committed in a caravan where the applicant and the boys had gone to stay for the night. Furthermore, in relation to counts one and two it was alleged that the applicant acted openly to the knowledge of the alleged victim while in relation to counts eight and nine he had acted secretly. The court concluded that as he should not have been tried on all the counts together his conviction should be quashed.

7. CROSS-EXAMINING THE ACCUSED ON HIS PREVIOUS CONVICTIONS OR HIS BAD CHARACTER

7.1 INTRODUCTION

Section 1 of the Criminal Justice (Evidence) Act 1924 changed the common law rule that an accused could not testify at his own trial. By making him competent the legislature was faced with a dilemma. Could the prosecution cross-examine the accused about his previous criminal record or his bad character? If the answer to this question was yes then this could have the unfair result of discouraging an innocent accused with a criminal record from giving evidence for fear that his record would influence the jury. However, if no cross-examination was allowed an accused would be free to falsely claim he was of good character or to attack the character of prosecution witnesses. He would be in a much better position than other witnesses. The only possible punishment he could face would be a perjury charge, which he might consider preferable to the charge he currently faced. Therefore, a compromise had to be reached. This compromise was set out in s.1(e) and s.1(f) of the 1924 Act. This chapter will consider these subsections.

Section 1(e) provides that:

> "A person charged and being a witness in pursuance of this Act may be asked any questions in cross-examination notwithstanding that it would tend to incriminate him as to the offence charged."

Section 1(f) provides as follows:

> "A person charged and called as a witness in pursuance of this Act shall not be asked, and if asked, shall not be required to answer, any question tending to show that he has committed or been convicted of or been charged with any offence other than that wherewith he is then charged, or is a bad character, unless-
>
> (i)   The proof that he has committed or been convicted of such other offences is admissible evidence to show that he is guilty of the offence wherewith he is then charged; or

(ii) He has personally or by his advocate asked questions of the witnesses for the prosecution with a view to establishing his own good character, or has given evidence of his good character, or the nature or the conduct of the defence is such as to involve imputations on the character of the prosecutor or the witnesses for the prosecution; or

(iii) He has given evidence against any other person charged with the same offence."

7.2 THE RELATIONSHIP BETWEEN THESE TWO SUBSECTIONS

At the outset the relationship between these two subsections needs to be considered. What happens if evidence is admissible under one section but prohibited under the other? For example, what if questions about an accused's previous criminal record (inadmissible under s.1(f)) tend to incriminate him (admissible under s.1(e))? The House of Lords discussed this question in *Jones v DPP* ([1962] A.C. 635) in relation to identical English legislation, the Criminal Evidence Act 1898. They held that there was no such difficulty in this case; however, had there been a conflict, s.1(f) would have prevailed. In other words, an accused can be asked any question relevant to his guilt once it is not prohibited by s.1(f). This prohibition has become known as an accused's "shield of protection".

7.3 THE SCOPE OF s.1(f)

Before considering the exceptions set out in s.1(f) the precise wording of its first paragraph needs to be considered because this sets out the scope of the prohibition. First, it is clear that s.1(f) only applies if the accused decides to testify. There is no obligation on him to do so and if he chooses not to s.1(f) does not come into play.

Secondly, the phrase "tending to show" has been held to have a particular meaning. The House of Lords in *Jones* established this. Here the appellant was convicted of murdering a girl guide. Three months earlier he had been convicted of raping another girl guide. There were similarities between the two cases. When the police questioned him about the murder he claimed to have an alibi. He said he was with his sister-in-law. Later, however, he changed his story and claimed to have been with a prostitute. He developed this story by saying that his wife was annoyed with him when he arrived home late and he detailed the row they had. At his rape trial the appellant tried to use the same alibi and gave an almost verbatim account of his wife's reaction. He also gave evidence in the murder trial. To justify his first alibi he said he had been in trouble with the police before and did not want to be in trouble again. The prosecution sought to cross-examine him about the similarities between the alibi he gave in this case and the one he used when he was in trouble before, to show he was not to be believed. The trial judge allowed them to do so and the appellant appealed claiming that this ruling breached the prohibition in s.1(f). The Court of Appeal upheld his conviction and the case went to the House of Lords on a question of law of general public importance.

The majority of the House of Lords held that the phrase "tending to show" meant tending to reveal for the first time. Here the accused admitted to being in trouble before during his examination-in-chief. Therefore, the jury already knew this by the time he was cross-examined. As Lord Reid stated: "If the jury already knew that the accused had been charged with an offence, a question inferring that he had been charged would add nothing and it would be absurd to prohibit it." Consequently, the House of Lords held that the questioning was permissible and his appeal was dismissed.

Section 1(f) prohibits questions that tend to show that an accused has been convicted of *or been charged with* any offence. Does this include an accused who, although previously charged with an offence, was acquitted of it? The House of Lords considered this issue in *Maxwell v DPP* ([1935] A.C. 309). Here the appellant doctor was charged with manslaughter. The prosecution alleged that he had carried out an illegal abortion. He gave evidence of his own good character, and the prosecution then cross-examined him on a previous similar charge of which he was acquitted.

Viscount Sankey L.C. commented that for questions to be admissible under s.1(f) they must be relevant to the issue of the accused's character. If not they were inadmissible. Here the fact that the accused had been previously charged and acquitted was irrelevant. It was also prejudicial as it could "lead the minds of the jury into false issues". Therefore, the accused's conviction was quashed.

However, Viscount Sankey L.C. made clear that this did not mean that an accused could never be cross-examined about previous acquittals. In certain circumstances such questioning may be admissible. He gave the example of an accused who could be asked whether he made the threats against his victim this time because he was angry with the victim for having brought an unfounded charge previously.

7.4 THE EXCEPTIONS TO THE PROHIBITION

There are four exceptions to the protection accorded by s.1(f).

An accused can be cross-examined about his previous convictions or his bad character if:

1. the information has already been admitted as similar fact evidence in the examination-in-chief; or
2. the accused has sought to establish his own good character in his defence; or
3. the accused has impugned the character of the prosecutor or of a prosecution witness; or
4. the accused has given evidence against a co-accused.

Each of these exceptions will be considered individually. However, one preliminary point needs to be highlighted. The evidence obtained under the first exception can be used to prove the guilt of the accused. In contrast, the evidence obtained under the other three exceptions can only be used to assess the credibility of the accused. This is an important theoretical distinction. In *People (AG) v Bond* ([1966] I.R. 214) the accused adduced evidence of his own good character and the prosecution cross-examined him about previous convictions. The Court of Criminal Appeal ordered a retrial because the trial judge failed to give the jury an adequate direction that this evidence could go to the accused's credibility only. However, in reality, once a correct direction is given it is difficult in practice to put a limit on the use a jury makes of a particular piece of information.

7.4.1 The information has already been admitted as similar fact evidence in the examination-in-chief

The last chapter indicated that misconduct evidence or similar fact evidence is admissible if its probative effect outweighs its prejudicial value. If such evidence is admissible the prosecution will in general present it when they are making their case.

As noted above the House of Lords in *Jones* interpreted the phrase "tending to show" as meaning tending to reveal for the first time. So if evidence is introduced when the prosecution are making their case then the prohibition in s.1(f) does not apply to it because it will not be revealed for the first time in cross-examination. This all means that this exception is rarely of use.

One situation where it is of assistance is when an accused's defence only becomes obvious to the prosecution when he is giving evidence. A good example of this is the decision in *R v Anderson* ([1988] Q.B. 678). Here the appellant, who was a member of the IRA, had been convicted of conspiracy to cause explosions likely to endanger life. When she was arrested false identity papers were discovered in her possession. At her trial she claimed to have had the documents because she was helping to smuggle escaped IRA prisoners out of the country. The prosecution were not forewarned that she was going to rely on this defence. To rebut it they sought leave to cross-examine her to establish that she had been wanted by the police before her arrest. The purpose of this cross-examination was to demonstrate that it was unlikely for a wanted person to be selected to assist other wanted people to escape. The prosecution were given leave by the trial judge and the accused admitted being a wanted person. The Court of Appeal upheld this decision.

7.4.2 The accused has sought to assert his own good character

The purpose of this exception is to prevent an accused exploiting the protection given to him by s.1(f). He cannot claim to be of good character if he is not. If he falsely claims to be of good character then it is only fair that he should be made answer questions about his bad character or previous convictions.

In *R v Samuel* ((1956) 40 Cr. App. R. 8) the Court of Appeal held that an accused charged with larceny by finding put his character in issue when he testified that previously when he found lost property he had returned it to its owner. Therefore, he could be cross-examined on his bad character. Similarly, in *R v Ferguson* ((1909) 2 Cr. App. R. 250) an accused who claimed that he attended mass regularly was held to put his character in issue.

An accused does not lose his shield if other defence witnesses give character evidence. This was established in *People (DPP) v Ferris* (unreported, June 10, 2002). Here the defence called two aunts of the complainant to give evidence. They testified that they had left their children alone with the accused and nothing had happened to them. The Court of Criminal Appeal held that this did not entitle the prosecution to cross-examine the accused as to his previous convictions. Fennelly J. pointed out that an accused was entitled to call character witnesses before the 1924 Act was introduced. Rather than cross-examining the accused, the prosecution could rebut this evidence by calling their own character witnesses. The 1924 Act was inapplicable to such circumstances.

7.4.3 The nature or the conduct of the defence is such as to involve imputations on the character of the prosecutor or the witnesses for the prosecution

This is a controversial exception. The main point of controversy is at what point the conduct of a defence involves imputations on the character of a prosecution witness such that an accused will lose his shield. Clearly, merely denying the charge is not enough even if the implication of this is that a prosecution witness is lying. But how far can an accused go in undermining the character of a prosecution witness? This issue has been considered on numerous occasions in this jurisdiction and in the UK. The respective approaches are radically different. Here the courts give the accused much more latitude in the conduct of his defence.

The UK has adopted a strict literal interpretation of their legislation. In *R v Hudson* ([1912] 2 K.B. 464) Lord Alverstone L.C.J. for the Court of Appeal held that the words must receive their ordinary and natural interpretation, and that it is not legitimate to qualify them by adding or inserting the words "unnecessarily", or "unjustifiably", or "for purposes other than that of developing the defence", or other similar words.

The House of Lords approved this judgment in *Selvey v DPP* ([1970] A.C. 304). The appellant was charged with buggery. The prosecution adduced medical evidence that the complainant had been sexually interfered with on the day in question and that indecent photographs had been found in the appellant's room by the police. The appellant denied the charge and testified that the complainant had told him that he had already committed buggery that day for £1 and would do the same again for money. The appellant denied knowing anything about the photos and suggested they had been planted on him. The trial judge allowed the prosecution to cross-examine the accused on his previous convictions, which included similar offences. In the appeal it was claimed that the trial judge should have exercised his discretion under s.1(f) in favour of the appellant and refused to permit the prosecution to cross-examine him on his previous convictions.

The House of Lords rejected this argument. They approved the decision in *Hudson* and held that the words of the statute should be given their ordinary meaning. Therefore, even where the nature of the defence necessarily involves the making of imputations on a prosecution witness an accused loses his shield. The court concluded that in most cases only mere denials of the prosecution's case could safeguard the accused's protection from cross-examination on previous convictions. They acknowledged that rape cases were an exception to this rule where an accused could assert that the complainant consented to the act without losing his shield.

Having strictly interpreted s.1(f) each of the Lords went on to accept that even though an accused loses his shield the trial judge retains a discretion to prohibit cross-examination on previous convictions in certain circumstances. Lord Hodson suggested that cross-examination on previous convictions might be disallowed as being unfair if, *e.g.* the accused's imputations on a prosecution witness were of minor significance when compared with the impact his previous convictions might have on his character.

This literal interpretation of s.1(f) has not been adopted in Ireland. In *AG v O'Shea* ([1931] I.R. 713) it was claimed that the nature of the defence's cross-examination of prosecution witnesses meant that the accused lost his shield. However, Kennedy C.J. held that the "testing of the truth and accuracy of their testimony by legitimate cross-examination, however severe, is not ... conduct of the defence as to involve imputations upon the character of the witnesses for the prosecution within Section 1(f)(ii)".

The leading case in Ireland is the Court of Criminal Appeal decision in *People (DPP) v McGrail* ([1990] 2 I.R. 38). Here the accused was charged with various offences under the Firearms Act 1964. The prosecution case was that the accused had been arrested whilst trying to escape from a flat which the gardaí had entered on foot of a search warrant. After he was arrested he made certain incriminating statements to the gardaí and told them where firearms were hidden. However, he refused to sign a garda note of the statements he made. During the trial, counsel for the accused put to various garda witnesses that the accused did not make the statements tendered, did not point out the place where the guns were hidden and that the gardaí were trying to convict him by inventing false verbal statements and other incriminating statements. The prosecution then applied to the trial judge for leave to cross-examine the accused on his previous convictions on the basis that the nature of the defence involved imputations on the character of prosecution witnesses. Counsel for the accused argued that whether or not the statements were made by his client was the central issue in the case and therefore he was entitled to challenge this evidence without exposing himself to cross-examination on his previous convictions. The trial judge gave the prosecution leave to cross-examine the accused and because of this he outlined his previous convictions in direct evidence. The accused was convicted and he applied to the Court of Criminal Appeal for leave to appeal.

Hederman J. gave the judgment of the court. He began by noting that every criminal trial involves an allegation about someone's character. Charging and presenting evidence against an accused is in effect an imputation against his character. Similarly, if the accused suggests that a prosecution witness is not to be believed that is an imputation against their character in the sense that it suggests they are lying. Therefore he stated:

> "It would be quite an intolerable situation if an accused person, in the conduct of the defence in cross-examining prosecution witnesses the veracity of whose evidence he was challenging, should be required to confine himself to suggesting a mistake or other innocent explanation to avoid the risk of having his character put in issue."

He contrasted this position with an accused who made an imputation against a prosecution witness independent of the facts in the case, *e.g.* if the defence claimed it was usual practice for the police to lie or make up evidence. It is only in these circumstances that an accused would lose his shield of protection. Any other reading of the section he concluded would be unfair.

> "This court is of the view that the principles of fair procedures must apply. A procedure which inhibits the accused from challenging the veracity of the evidence against him at the risk of having his own previous character put in evidence is not a fair procedure. The gratuitous introduction of material by way of cross-examination or otherwise to show that the witness for the prosecution has a general

bad character, divorced from the facts of the case at hearing, is a different matter."

People (AG) v Coleman ([1945] I.R. 237) is an example of a case where the defence would appear to have satisfied the above threshold. Here the appellant was convicted of performing a criminal abortion. There were two main prosecution witnesses, the woman who had the abortion and her husband. The defence made a number of allegations against these witnesses. The most significant of these was that the husband had committed a similar offence himself. The trial judge permitted the prosecution to cross-examine the appellant on his previous convictions. The Court of Criminal Appeal upheld this ruling because the imputation was not that the husband had carried out the offence that the accused was charged with but that he had carried out a similar offence (independent from the case against the accused).

7.4.4 The accused has given evidence against any other person charged with the same offence

There has been little discussion of this exception in this jurisdiction. In the UK the most important issue under this exception is what does "given evidence against" mean? The House of Lords considered this question in *Murdoch v Taylor* ([1965] 1 All E.R. 406). The appellant Murdoch had a criminal record. He was tried with another man Lynch who did not. They were charged with receiving stolen goods. Murdoch gave evidence that he had nothing to do with the stolen goods, that he did not know what was in a certain box in Lynch's possession and that the transaction was entirely Lynch's idea. The trial judge held that Lynch's counsel was entitled to cross-examine Murdoch on his previous convictions.

The House of Lords upheld this ruling. They held that "evidence against" means evidence which supports the prosecution's case in a material respect or undermines the defence of the co-accused. It is not necessary for the witness to have any hostile intent. The House of Lords also held that once the trial judge has ruled that the witness has given evidence against a co-accused he has no discretion whether or not to allow him to be cross-examined on his previous convictions. This is in contrast to the previous two exceptions. This distinction was justified on the basis that a co-accused has a right to defend himself against conviction and this right cannot be fettered in any way.

In *R v Varley* ([1982] 2 All E.R. 519) the appellant and a man named Dibble were jointly charged with robbery. At their trial Dibble admitted that they had both participated in the robbery but claimed that he had been forced to do so because the appellant had made threats on his life. The appellant denied he had taken part in the robbery and asserted that Dibble's evidence was untrue. On that basis the trial judge gave Dibble's counsel leave to cross-examine the appellant on his previous convictions. In his appeal the appellant contended that his evidence was not evidence against Dibble and therefore leave to cross-examine him should not have been granted. The Court of Appeal upheld the trial judge's ruling and in doing so they laid down the following guidelines:

> "1) If it is established that a person jointly charged has given evidence against a co-accused that defendant has a right to cross-examine the other as to previous convictions and the trial judge has no discretion to refuse an application.
>
> 2) Such evidence may be given either in chief or during cross-examination.
>
> 3) It has to be objectively decided whether the evidence either supports the prosecution case in a material respect or undermines the defence of the co-accused. A hostile intent is irrelevant.
>
> 4) If consideration has to be given to the undermining of the others' defence care must be taken to see that the evidence clearly undermines the defence. Inconvenience to or inconsistency with the other's defence is not of itself sufficient.
>
> 5) Mere denial of participation in a joint venture is not of itself sufficient to rank as evidence against the co-defendant. For the proviso to apply, such denial must lead to the conclusion that if the witness did not participate then it must have been the other who did.
>
> 6) Where one defendant asserts or in due course would assert one view of the joint venture which is directly contradicted by the other, such contradiction may be evidence against the co-defendant."

8. THE RULE AGAINST HEARSAY

8.1 INTRODUCTION

The rule against hearsay is one of the more complicated evidential rules. It is difficult to set out a precise definition of the rule. In *Cullen v Clarke* ([1963] I.R. 368) Kingsmill Moore J. set out one of the best descriptions of the rule:

> "[T]here is *no* general rule of evidence to the effect that a witness may not testify as to the words spoken by a person who is not produced as a witness. There *is* a general rule, subject to many exceptions, that evidence of the speaking of such words is inadmissible to prove the truth of the facts which they assert; the reasons being that the truth of the words cannot be tested by cross-examination and has not the sanctity of an oath. This is the rule known as the rule against hearsay."

This quotation contains a number of very important elements. First, it begins by stating what the rule is not. It is not a rule that prohibits witnesses testifying about what they heard from someone else. Such evidence is admissible. It is only inadmissible if it is sought to be admitted to prove the truth of what was overheard. For example, witness X can testify that person Y told him it rained on a particular night. That is admissible. However, it is not admissible as proof that it actually rained on that night.

A good example of the rule in practice is the decision in *Subramanian v DPP* ([1956] 1 W.L.R. 965). Here the accused was charged with the unlawful possession of ammunition. He claimed that terrorists had captured him and that he had acted under duress. He tried to introduce evidence of his capture and what the terrorists had said to him. However, the trial judge ruled that such conversations were inadmissible as hearsay unless the terrorists were called to give evidence. The Privy Council overturned this on appeal. They held that a statement:

> "is hearsay and inadmissible when the object of the evidence is to establish the truth of what is contained in the statement. It is not hearsay and is admissible when it is proposed to establish by the evidence, not the truth of the statement but the fact that it was made".

63

Here it was irrelevant whether the statements made by terrorists to the appellant were true or not. Regardless of their truth, if the appellant had believed them, he may have been entitled to rely on the defence of duress. It would have been different if the statements were introduced into the court as evidence that the terrorists actually intended to kill him.

8.2 THE RATIONALE FOR THE RULE

There are several reasons why the rule came into existence. The most important reason is that whoever made the statement should testify so they are available for cross-examination. In our adversarial system cross-examination is the primary method used to test evidence. The right of an accused to cross-examine his accuser may be considered to be a constituent of a constitutional right. In *Re Haughey* ([1971] I.R. 217 at 264) O'Dálaigh J. held that the right to fair procedures guaranteed by Art.40.3 of the Constitution included a right that the defendant be permitted to cross-examine his accusers.

There are several other reasons why the rule exists:

a) A witness should give evidence in court so that the judge and/or jury can observe his demeanour.
b) Sworn testimony is considered best evidence.
c) Second-hand information is more likely to be inaccurate.
d) Without the rule a litigant could try to improve his chances of success by repeating his side of the story to many people and have them all testify on his behalf.
e) Trials would be longer and consequently more expensive if the rule did not exist.

8.3 THE DISADVANTAGES OF THE RULE

There are many disadvantages of the rule against hearsay. It can lead to highly probative evidence being ruled inadmissible, *e.g.* the evidence of a dead or unidentified person. This could result in an injustice being done. For example in *R v Gray* ((1841) 2 Cr. & Dix. 129) a deathbed confession by a third party that he and not the accused had committed the murder was held to be inadmissible evidence under the hearsay rule. The rule can also lead to extra expense, as witnesses have to turn up to prove certain pieces of evidence.

8.4 EXAMPLES OF THE RULE

This section will examine oral statements, written statements and then it will discuss the controversial area of implied assertions.

8.4.1 Oral statements

It is clear that the rule against hearsay applies to oral statements. In *Teper v R* ([1952] A.C. 480) the accused was convicted of maliciously setting fire to a shop with intent to defraud his insurance company. At his trial a policeman gave evidence that he had heard a woman saying: "Your place burning and you are going away from the fire", and immediately noticed a black car coming from the direction of the fire with a man in it, who resembled the accused. The woman was never identified and consequently was not a witness. Both sides accepted that the policeman was further than a furlong away from the shop and the incident happened at least 26 minutes after the fire started. The Privy Counsel allowed the appeal. They held that the statement by the woman was inadmissible hearsay evidence.

In Ireland the case of *Cullen v Clarke* provides a good example of the rule. The applicant was injured while employed as a builder's labourer. He sought to obtain compensation under workmen's compensation legislation. To be successful in this claim he had to show he was incapacitated because of the injury. He sought to do this by quoting statements from several prospective employers as to why they would not give him work. The Supreme Court held that as he was relying on the truth of such statements they were hearsay.

8.4.2 Written statements

It is also clear that the rule against hearsay applies to written statements. In *Myers v DPP* ([1965] A.C. 1001) the case against the accused was somewhat convoluted. It was claimed that the accused stole cars, purchased similar wrecked cars and then transferred to the stolen cars the engine and chassis numbers of the wrecked cars so they matched the numbers in the logbooks of the wrecked cars. He then sold on the stolen cars with the wrecked cars' logbooks. However, each of the stolen cars had another identifying number i.e. the cylinder block number. This number was indelibly stamped on the engine and could not be changed. The prosecution case relied on the fact that there was a mismatch between this number and the other altered numbers. To prove their case the prosecution called witnesses from the car manufacturers who kept records of all three numbers. The problem was that these records were actually compiled by various unidentified workmen as the cars were assembled in the factory. The defence claimed that this evidence was inadmissible hearsay. The trial judge and the Court of Criminal Appeal rejected this argument. However, the majority of the House of Lords accepted it. They held that the only purpose of admitting the records was to show what they recorded to be true. Therefore, the records were hearsay. The result in this case would not be the same today because the Criminal Evidence Act 1992 makes these types of records admissible.

8.4.3 Implied assertions original evidence or inadmissible hearsay?

This is quite a controversial area and the courts in this jurisdiction have not really considered it. The controversy can be explained by reference to the quotation from *Cullen v Clarke* at the beginning of this chapter. Kingsmill Moore J. said: "evidence of the speaking of such words is inadmissible to prove the truth of *the facts which they assert*" (emphasis added). It is clear from this that the rule applies to assertive factual statements. But what if the impugned words do not assert anything in particular but rather only imply something? Can this distinction be used to limit the scope of the rule against hearsay? It appears that the answer to this question is yes, however, the case law is not entirely consistent on this point.

One of the first cases on this point was the decision in *Wright v Doe d Tatham* ((1838) 7 Ad. & E 313). This case concerned a dispute about whether a testator had the capacity to make a will. The party seeking to uphold the will sought to introduce into evidence letters written to the deceased, which implied that he was sane. The court held that the rule against hearsay could not be avoided in this way:

> "those letters may be considered in this respect to be on the same footing as if they had contained a direct and positive statement that he was competent. For this purpose they are mere hearsay evidence, statements of the writers, not on oath, of the truth of the matter in question".

However, a different conclusion was reached in *Ratten v R* ([1972] A.C. 378). The appellant was convicted of murdering his wife by shooting her with a shotgun. He claimed that the gun went off accidentally as he was cleaning it. At his trial a telephone operator from the local exchange gave evidence of receiving a call from the appellant's house. The call was from a female who, in a hysterical voice said: "Get me the police, please". The defendant had denied that a phone call had been made from his house at this time. The statement was held to be admissible as original evidence. On the one hand this is uncontroversial; the accused claimed no phone call had been made so the operator's evidence was clearly relevant, regardless of the truth of what the caller had said to her. However, the statement also appears to have been held admissible even though it implied that the woman was in a state of fear and that the jury could infer from it that her death was not an accident. This reasoning, therefore, clearly suggests that implied assertions are not covered by the rule against hearsay.

Similar reasoning was applied in *R v Rice* ([1963] 1 Q.B. 857). The appellant was convicted of conspiracy to steal cars. The prosecution case involved proving that the appellant took a flight with another man. They introduced into evidence a used airline ticket with the names of Rice and the other man on it, which had been retained by an airline representative as passengers had boarded a flight. On appeal the appellant claimed, *inter alia*, that the ticket was hearsay as it was used to show he had taken the flight in question. The Court of Criminal Appeal rejected this and held the tickets admissible. They held "that the production of the ticket was a fact from which the jury might infer that probably two people had flown on the particular flight and...that the passengers bore the surnames which were written on the ticket."

These cases can be contrasted with the House of Lords decision in *R v Kearley* ([1992] 2 W.L.R. 656). The police suspected that Kearley was selling illegal drugs. They found drugs hidden in a rabbit hutch in his garden but not in sufficient quantities to raise the inference that he possessed the drugs for the purpose of supply. While on the premises, the police intercepted 15 telephone calls. Three of the callers asked for Kearley and for drugs. None of these callers appeared as witnesses at the trial. The prosecution proposed to call the police officer who had taken these calls to give evidence of them. It was argued that the request for the drugs implied a belief, on the part of the caller, that Kearley sold drugs and that this was relevant to the facts in issue. The trial judge and the Court of Criminal Appeal held that the words spoken were admissible. However, the Court of Criminal Appeal certified a point of law of public importance to the House of Lords. In essence they were asked if evidence may be adduced at a trial of words spoken, not for the purpose of establishing the truth of any fact narrated by the words, but of inviting the jury to draw an inference from the fact that the words were spoken. The majority of the House of Lords decided that these calls implied that the callers believed that the defendant was a dealer in drugs. They held such a belief was irrelevant to the charges. But even if relevant, implied assertions could not be treated differently to express assertions and that both equally fell within the hearsay exception. There was a strong dissent by Lord Griffiths and Lord Browne-Wilkinson, saying that to apply the hearsay rule here hampers effective prosecution by excluding evidence that everyone agrees is highly probative and very creditworthy, since it comes from unprompted sources.

8.5 EXCEPTIONS TO THE HEARSAY RULE

There are numerous exceptions to the hearsay rule. They can be divided into two broad categories, those created by the common law and those created by statute. Both categories will be dealt with in turn.

8.5.1 Exceptions at common law

8.5.1.1 Confessions
Confession evidence is an extremely important exception to the rule against hearsay and will be dealt with separately in the next chapter.

8.5.1.2 The doctrine of res gestae
This is a Latin phrase, which means the remarks which relate to a particular act. Essentially what we are concerned with here is a statement which is so intertwined with an act that it can be said to be admissible as part of that act. Without the statement the act would not make sense. Four particular situations are covered by this exception. Each will be considered individually; however, it is worth pointing out that in *Homes v Newman* ([1931] 2 Ch. 112) Lord Tomlin described the doctrine as "a phrase adopted to provide a respectable

legal cloak for a variety of cases to which no formulae of precision can be applied".

The four situations are:

(i) spontaneous statements made by a participant in an act;
(ii) spontaneous statements, which accompany and explain a relevant act;
(iii) spontaneous statements showing the maker's contemporaneous state of mind;
(iv) spontaneous statements of contemporaneous physical sensation felt by the maker.

The situations have some factors in common. First, as the above explanation suggests, the statement must be contemporaneous with the act. Secondly, the maker of the statement must not be available to give evidence. Finally, as they are exceptions to the hearsay rule, the statements are admissible as proof of the truth of their contents.

(i) Spontaneous statements made by a participant in an act
Historically this category was interpreted quite restrictively in that the statement had to form part of the event. One of the more stark illustrations of this strict requirement is the decision in *R v Beddingfield* ((1879) 14 Cox C.C. 341). The accused was charged with murdering a woman by cutting her throat. He claimed that she committed suicide. The evidence was that she had come out of a room with her throat cut and upon meeting two women said: "See what Harry has done!" She died a few minutes later and the accused was found to be the only person in the room. The court held that the statement overheard by the women was inadmissible as "it was not part of anything done, or something said while something was being done, but something said after something done".

Fortunately in modern times the courts have moved away from this rather rigid approach. Now their attitude is more in keeping with the underlying logic of the exception. The exception came about because it was felt that such statements were more likely to be true. Therefore, now the courts are more concerned with whether the circumstances of the statement are such that the possibility that it has been fabricated or made in error can be disregarded.

A good example of this approach is the judgment of Lord Wilberforce in *Ratten v R*. The statement "Get me the police, please" was held by Lord Wilberforce to be admissible original evidence. However, he went on in his judgment to assume that it was in fact hearsay. He concluded that if it had been hearsay, it would have been admitted under the *res gestae* exception. According to him, "the test should not be the uncertain one of whether the making of the statement was in some sense part of the event or transaction". Instead a judge must be satisfied that:

> "the statement was so clearly made in circumstances of spontaneity or involvement in the event that the possibility of concoction can be disregarded. Conversely, if he considers that the statement was made by way of narrative of a detached prior event so that the speaker was so disengaged from it as to be able to construct or adapt his account, he should exclude it."

The House of Lords endorsed this reasoning in *R v Andrews* ([1987] A.C. 281). The appellant and another man entered the victim's flat and stabbed him. The victim managed to make his way to the flat below to get help. The police arrived a few minutes later and the victim told them who had stabbed him. He subsequently lost consciousness and died two months later. The appellant was tried for murder and the victim's statement was admitted in evidence. The accused appealed on the basis that it should not have been admitted under the doctrine of *res gestae*. The House of Lords confirmed Lord Wilberforce's *obiter dictum* in *Ratten*. Lord Ackner held that the trial judge must ask himself if the possibility of concoction or distortion can be disregarded. To answer that question the judge must satisfy himself that the event was so unusual "as to dominate the thoughts of the victim, so that his utterance was an instinctive reaction to that event, thus giving no real opportunity for reasoned reflection". Here the evidence satisfied this test.

The House of Lords also commented that they felt *Beddingfield* was wrongly decided. Indeed, they considered that there could "hardly be a case where the words uttered carried more clearly the mark of spontaneity and intense involvement".

(ii) Spontaneous statements, which accompany and explain a relevant act

The act in question must be relevant to a fact in issue in the case. The person who performs the act must have made the statement and it must explain why the act was done.

In *R v Edwards* ((1872) 12 Cox C.C.) the accused was charged with murdering his wife. Prior to her death she had left a knife and an axe in a neighbour's house. On the basis of this exception the trial judge allowed the neighbour to testify that when doing so the wife said: "My husband always threatens me with these and when they're out of the way I feel safer."

(iii) Spontaneous statements showing the maker's contemporaneous state of mind

The state of mind of the declarant must be relevant to a fact in issue. The statement must be made contemporaneously with the state of mind and must show the state of mind.

In *R v Vincent* ((1840) 9 C. & P. 275) it was claimed that general alarm had been caused at a public meeting. The trial judge allowed a police officer to give evidence that a number of people had told him the meeting had made them fearful and apprehensive.

(iv) Spontaneous statements of contemporaneous physical sensation felt by the maker

The physical sensation must be relevant to a fact in issue. The requirement that the sensation be contemporaneous is quite lax under this heading; for example, according to *R v Black* ((1922) 16 Cr. App. Rep. 118) it would be sufficient if the sensation were felt the day before the statement was made. The statement is admissible to prove the fact of the sensation but not its cause.

8.5.1.3 Statements or declarations of deceased persons

Certain statements or declarations made by persons, since deceased, are admissible as an exception to the hearsay rule. It has to be the case that the evidence would be admissible if the deceased were alive to testify.

(i) Dying declarations in relation to the cause of death

These declarations are only admissible in murder or manslaughter cases. The declarant must have been the victim of the homicide. The declaration can be made orally or in writing. The historic rationale for this exception is the Christian view that no one would want to die with a lie on their conscience, so a declaration in these circumstances is more than likely true. Therefore, the person must be under a "settled hopeless expectation" of death when he made the statement.

There has been a significant amount of case law on this point. In *R v Andrews* the deceased did not know he was going to die, therefore, his statement to the police was inadmissible under this exception. In *R v Mooney* ((1851) 5 Cox C.C. 318) the deceased's doctor told her she was seriously ill and her clergyman told her to prepare for death. However, she had not told anyone that she knew she was dying and, therefore, the court held that her declaration was inadmissible.

(ii) Declarations of a deceased person against proprietary or pecuniary interest

Such a statement must be against interest at the time it was made. The rationale for admitting these statements is similar to the justification for admitting confessions. A statement made against the maker's interest is more likely to be true as there is no incentive to lie. Therefore, the maker must be aware that the statement is against his interest when he makes it. An example of this exception in practice is *Flood v Russell* ((1891) 29 L.R. I.R. 91). Here a wife made a statement that her husband had made a will which left her a life estate in certain property. The statement by the wife was against her interest, as without the will she would have been entitled to more than a life estate. Therefore, her statement was admissible.

(iii) Declarations of a deceased person made in the course of duty

The deceased person must have made these declarations in pursuance of a duty owed by him to someone else. The rationale for this exception is that as they were made in the course of work there would have been little motive to lie. He must have recorded his own performance of an act. The declaration must have been made contemporaneously with the act. Only statements of facts not opinions are admissible.

(iv) Declarations of a deceased person relating to pedigree

The declaration must have been made on a matter of pedigree, *e.g.* the date of someone's birth, death or marriage, whether someone died testate or intestate or whether a child was legitimate or not. The declarant must have been a blood relative, or a spouse of a blood relative, of the person whose pedigree is at issue. There is no requirement that the declarant have personal knowledge of the subject matter of the declaration. The declaration must have been made before the dispute arose.

(v) Declarations of deceased persons as to public and general rights
These declarations must concern a public or general right, not a private right. The declaration must have been made before the dispute arose. In *Giant's Causeway Co. Ltd v AG* ([1905] 5 New. Ir. Rep. 301), an original Ordnance Survey map was admitted to establish the existence of a public right of way.

(vi) Declarations by a deceased testator as to the contents of his will
Declarations by a deceased testator are admissible if they are necessary to explain the contents of his will. They can be made either before or after the will is executed. In *In the Goods of Ball* ((1890) 25 L.R. Ir. 556) the testator wrote on the first page of a copy of his will that he had substituted the copy for the original. The court held that this statement was admissible to prove the contents of the will.

8.5.1.4 Statements contained in public documents
In certain circumstances statements in public documents are admissible as an exception to the hearsay rule. They are regarded as prima facie evidence of the facts they contain. The rationale for the rule is that public officers can be expected to carry out their functions diligently when their work is open to public inspection. This rationale explains some of the requirements of the exception. First, to qualify under this exception the document must have been made by a public officer in the exercise of a duty to enquire into the information recorded. Secondly, it must have been intended that the document be retained for public inspection. Finally, it must contain a matter of public interest.

8.5.2 Statutory exceptions

Several acts of the legislature have made certain categories of evidence admissible which otherwise would be prohibited on the basis of the rule against hearsay. Two Acts in particular will be considered: the Criminal Evidence Act 1992 and the Children Act 1997.

8.5.2.1 The Criminal Evidence Act 1992

This Act introduces a new exception to the rule against hearsay. However, the Act only applies to criminal proceedings. Section 5 of the Act provides that information in a document made in the ordinary course of business is admissible as evidence of any fact contained therein. According to s.8 the court has discretion to exclude any document if it is in the interests of justice. Section 8(2) lists the factors that the court can take into account in deciding whether or not to exercise this discretion. They include whether the information is reliable, authentic and that its admission or exclusion will result in unfairness to the accused. Section 30 provides that copies of a document may be produced in evidence (whether or not the original is in existence), authenticated in such a manner as the court may approve.

8.5.2.2 The Children Act 1997

Prior to the introduction of this Act, proceedings that dealt with the welfare of children were governed by the Supreme Court decision in *Eastern Health Board v M.K.* ([1999] 2 I.R. 99). This decision will be considered as it may still be of relevance if the correct interpretation of the Act is in dispute. Here the respondents were the parents of three children which the applicant sought to make wards of court. The applicant claimed that one of the children had been sexually abused by his father. To establish this they sought to introduce hearsay evidence. The child in question did not give evidence, instead a social worker and a speech therapist gave evidence of what the child had said to them. A videotape of the interview with the social worker was also introduced in evidence. The High Court admitted the evidence and the children were taken into wardship. Costello P. made it clear that if the hearsay evidence had been excluded the other evidence in the case would not have justified the making of the order.

The respondents appealed to the Supreme Court claiming the hearsay evidence should not have been admitted. The Supreme Court held that in general hearsay evidence was admissible in wardship proceedings due to the special nature of those proceedings. They are inquisitorial in nature and primarily concerned with the welfare of the child. However, for the evidence to be so admissible certain criteria must be satisfied, these were not satisfied in this case and, therefore, the evidence should not have been admitted. According to Keane J. the trial judge should begin by examining whether the child was competent to give evidence. He should then consider whether the trauma of giving evidence would make it undesirable for the child to do so. Here the trial judge had only considered the trauma issue, he had not taken into account whether the child was competent to give evidence. The Supreme Court also held that the trial judge failed to consider whether or not the evidence was sufficiently reliable before he admitted it.

The Children Act 1997 now governs this area. Section 23(1) of the Act provides that a statement made by a child is admissible notwithstanding the hearsay rule where the court considers that (a) the child is unable to give evidence by reason of age, or (b) the giving of oral evidence by the child would not be in the interest of the welfare of the child. However, s.23(2) provides that such a statement will not be admitted if the court is of the opinion that it would not be in the interests of justice to admit it. In considering this issue the court will have regard to all the circumstances of the case including any risk that the admission will result in unfairness to any of the parties.

Once the statement is admissible the court must then assess what weight to attach to it. Section 24(1) of the Act provides that in considering the weight to attach to any statement the court should have regard to all the circumstances from which any inference can reasonably be drawn as to its accuracy. Five factors that the court should have particular regard to are set out in s.24(2):

1. whether the original statement was made contemporaneously with the occurrence or existence of the matters stated;
2. whether the evidence involves multiple hearsay;
3. whether any person involved has any motive to conceal or misrepresent matters;
4. whether the original statement was an edited account or was made in collaboration with another for a particular purpose; and
5. whether the circumstances in which the evidence is adduced as hearsay are such as to suggest an attempt to prevent the proper evaluation of its weight.

9. CONFESSION EVIDENCE

9.1 INTRODUCTION

Confessions are one of the most controversial exceptions to the hearsay rule. They are admissible because they are viewed as inculpatory statements, *i.e.* statements made against self-interest, so they are considered more likely to be true. However, an accused at trial will often claim that he never made the confession, that he was forced to make it or that it should be held inadmissible for some other reason. In *R v Thompson* ([1893] 2 Q.B. 12) Cave J. declared:

> "I always suspect these confessions, which are supposed to be the offspring of penitence and remorse, and which nevertheless are repudiated by the prisoner at the trial."

Therefore, the main legal issue to be dealt with here is: when is a confession admissible? It should be remembered that the burden of proving that a confession should is admissible is on the prosecution. In examining this issue five main questions will be examined:

1. Was the confession voluntary or involuntary?
2. Were the accused's constitutional rights infringed?
3. Was there a breach of the Judges' Rules?
4. Was there a breach of the Criminal Justice Act (Treatment of Persons in Custody in Garda Síochána Stations) Regulations 1987?
5. Did the way in which the confession was obtained breach principles of fundamental fairness?

9.2 WAS THE CONFESSION VOLUNTARY OR INVOLUNTARY?

If a confession was not voluntarily given it is automatically inadmissible, the trial judge has no discretion to allow it. The burden is on the prosecution to establish beyond reasonable doubt that a confession is voluntary. Obviously voluntariness in this context has a specific meaning, as there are numerous arrestees who would rather not have been caught or interrogated at all. The test for voluntariness used by the courts has developed over the years.

Traditionally the courts excluded confessions which had been obtained by threats or promises (jointly known as inducements) made by persons in authority. So, in the UK the leading definition of voluntariness is that set out in *Ibrahim v R* ([1914] A.C. 599) where Lord Sumner stated: "a voluntary statement, in the sense that it has not been obtained from him either by fear of prejudice or hope of advantage exercised or held out by a person in authority". In a similar vein in this jurisdiction Fitzgibbon J. in *State v Treanor* ([1924] 2 I.R. 193) declared: "[a] confession made to any person under the influence of a promise or threat held out by a person in authority, calculated to induce a confession, is inadmissible". There are numerous examples of this test for voluntariness being applied by the courts.

9.2.1 Threats, promises or inducements

In *AG v Cleary* ((1938) 72 I.L.T.R. 84) the accused was charged with the murder of her baby. The gardaí threatened to take her to a doctor who would be able to tell if she recently had a baby and whether it had been born alive. This threat was held to make her confession involuntary and consequently inadmissible.

In *R v Richards* ([1967] 1 All E.R. 829) a policeman said to the appellant: "I think it would be better if you made a statement and told me exactly what happened". The Court of Appeal found that this statement amounted to an inducement so the accused's confession was held inadmissible.

In *R v Northam* ((1967) 52 Cr. App. R. 97) the appellant, while awaiting trial on a number of charges of housebreaking, was questioned by the police about another offence of housebreaking. He asked a police officer if he could have this offence taken into consideration at the pending trial. The officer said the police would have no problem with this. The accused then confessed. Subsequently he was tried separately for this particular offence. His conviction was set aside on the ground that the police officer's reply to his question constituted an inducement and therefore his confession should not have been admitted in evidence.

In *People (AG) v Flynn* ([1963] I.R. 255) the appellant had been arrested and was questioned by the gardaí. After two hours of being totally uncooperative he was left in a cell and the interviewing garda went for lunch. A sergeant brought the appellant his lunch and had a conversation with him and said that it would be just as well if he told the truth. The appellant made a confession after lunch. The trial judge admitted the statement and the appellant was convicted. The Court of Criminal Appeal quashed the appellant's conviction.

According to Davitt P. it was not possible to be sure the statement was voluntarily made without any inducement.

In *People DPP v Hoey* ([1987] I.R. 637) the police searched the accused's family's house and found firearms and ammunition. Initially the accused fled; however, he subsequently surrendered himself at a garda station. He was arrested under s.30 of the Offences Against the State Act 1939 and was questioned for extensive periods, but he remained silent. A garda then said: "It must be somebody in the house. Will I have to get some member to go up to your family and find out from them if anybody at 78 Rossmore Avenue is going to take responsibility for the property?" The accused then made a confession. The Supreme Court held that the garda's statement was an inducement, which rendered his confession inadmissible. The accused believed his family would not be interrogated if he took responsibility for the firearms.

In *People (DPP) v Geoghegan* (unreported, November 18, 2003) the court directed that the accused should be acquitted. The main evidence against the accused was a confession he had made after the gardaí promised him that if he confessed he would only be charged with assault and would get bail. In fact he was charged with murder.

9.2.2 A broader test

Recently the courts have accepted that a confession could be involuntary for reasons other than threats or promises. For example, simply being interrogated for hours by the gardaí could make a confession involuntary. As Griffin J. pointed out in *People (DPP) v Shaw* ([1982] I.R.1): "The circumstances which will make a statement inadmissible for lack of voluntariness are so varied that it would be impossible to enumerate or categorize them fully."

Oppression/Oppressive questioning

One category that has emerged with the increased use of prolonged interrogations by the gardaí is a test of oppression or oppressive questioning. For example, in *People (DPP) v Madden* ([1977] I.R. 336) O'Higgins C.J. accepted that: "it would be possible for a protracted period of detention, coupled with persistent interviewing or interrogation, to constitute oppression".

The English Court of Appeal has considered the meaning of oppressive questioning on several occasions. In *R v Priestly* ((1966) 51 Cr. App. R. 1) oppressive questioning was explained as "something which tends to sap, and has sapped, that free will which must exist before a confession is voluntary". Similarly in *R v Prager* ((1972) 56 Cr. App. R. 151) it was described as "questioning which by its nature, duration or other attendant circumstances (including the fact of custody) excites hopes (such as the hope of release) or fears, or so affects the mind of the subject that his will crumbles and he speaks when otherwise he would have stayed silent".

The Court of Criminal Appeal approved both of these definitions in *People (DPP) v McNally & Breathnach* ((1981) 2 Frewen 43). Here the applicants had been convicted of the Sallins train robbery in the Special Criminal Court. The only evidence against them was confessions they had made in garda custody. The second applicant made his confession after being in custody for approximately 40 hours. During that time he was interrogated extensively, allowed very little sleep and was denied access to his solicitor. The Court of Criminal Appeal held that these circumstances were oppressive.

A subjective test

The test of establishing whether the confession is voluntary or not is a subjective one. The courts are concerned with the effect the inducement or oppressive questioning has on the mind of the accused. They are not concerned with how a reasonable person would have reacted or what the intention of the garda was. The Court of Criminal Appeal established this in *People (DPP) v Pringle* ((1981) 2 Frewen 57). The appellant was convicted of capital murder. He had been arrested under s.30 of the Offences Against the State Act 1939 and was interrogated extensively over a weekend. At one point he said: "I know that you know I was involved, but on the advice of my solicitor I am saying nothing and you are going to have to prove it all the way". The Special Criminal Court held that these words were in effect a confession and, therefore, the statement was admissible. One of the questions for the Court of Criminal Appeal was whether this statement should have been excluded on the basis that it was not made voluntarily.

O'Higgins C.J. held that the test for oppression was subjective:

> "what may be oppressive as regards a child, an invalid, or an old man or someone inexperienced in the ways of the world may turn out not to be oppressive when one finds that the accused is of tough character and an experienced man of the world".

The court noted that prior to making the statement the applicant had been interrogated for lengthy periods by the gardaí. However, he had spoken to his solicitor on five occasions before he made the statement. Furthermore, the judge noted that the accused was a 42-year-old fisherman, not unused to conditions of physical hardship. Therefore, applying the subjective test the confession was held to be voluntary and was admissible.

The Irish courts have subsequently applied this subjective test consistently. In *People DPP v Hoey* ([1987] I.R. 637) the Supreme Court held that the test was subjective. The issue is what effect the inducement had on the person to whom it was put, not what the garda intended.

The inducement or oppression must have come from someone in authority

In the majority of cases the threat, inducement or oppression in question will have come from a member of the Garda Síochána and, therefore, there will be no difficulty with this requirement. However, in certain circumstances it may have come from another source. In those situations the question may arise as to whether the person is someone in authority.

Various categories of persons have been held to satisfy this requirement for the purposes of the rule. For example a headmistress has been held to be a person in authority in relation to schoolgirls (*R v McLintock* [1962] Crim. L.Rep. 549). In *People v Murphy* ([1946] I.R. 236) a garda got a civilian to help him. He said to the accused: "Go with the garda, it's for your own good". This statement was made in the presence of the garda who did not object to it. The court held the civilian to be a person in authority for the purposes of the rule.

In *Deokinian v R* ([1969] 1 A.C. 20) the appellant made a confession to a trusted friend while in a police cell. The trusted friend was someone who was known to be "close to the police". In fact he had been put in the cell by the police to obtain information from the accused. The appellant argued that someone who was known to be close to the police should be treated as someone in authority, for the purposes of the rule. The Privy Council rejected this argument on the basis that here, the individual made the statement to a trusted friend who just happened to be close to the police. The appellant did not regard him as a person in authority. However, the implication of the judgment was that if someone is known by an accused to be close to the police, that person could be considered as a person in authority.

In *People (DPP) v McCann* ([1998] 4 I.R. 397) the Court of Criminal Appeal held that the applicant's brothers were not persons in authority. He was arrested on suspicion of starting a fire at his home in which his wife and child died. He told his brothers that he and his wife had a suicide pact. The brothers asked the applicant to repeat what he had told them to the gardaí, which he did. Therefore, the confession was admissible as the threat or inducement had not come from someone in authority.

There must be a causative link between the threat, inducement or oppression and the confession made
The accused must prove that the taint actually caused him to make the confession.

A good example of this rule in practice is *Pringle*. Here the gardaí threatened the accused that if he did not account for his movements on the day in question his girlfriend would be charged as an accessory. He consulted with his solicitor after this threat was made and was assured that this was impossible. The accused accepted his solicitor's word. Therefore, his subsequent confession was causatively unrelated to that threat. It had not induced him to make the statement.

9.3 WERE THE ACCUSED'S CONSTITUTIONAL RIGHTS INFRINGED?

Confessions obtained as a result of a breach of a constitutional right are also automatically inadmissible. The rule excluding evidence obtained in breach of constitutional rights was first established in the context of real evidence in the leading case of *People (AG) v O'Brien* ([1965] I.R. 142). Here Walsh J. stated: "evidence obtained in deliberate and conscious violation of the constitutional rights of an accused should, save in extraordinary excusing circumstances, be absolutely inadmissible".

This case dealt with unconstitutionally obtained real evidence and did not relate to confessions. In *People (DPP) v Shaw* ([1982] 1 I.R. 1) a majority of the Supreme Court held that the *O'Brien* principle should not be extended to confessions. However, a different view was expressed in *People (DPP) v Madden* ([1977] I.R. 336). Here the applicant had been detained for questioning under s.30 of

The Offences Against The State Act 1939. His detention continued beyond the time limit allowed in the Act. The Court of Criminal Appeal held that a confession made by him during this unlawful period of detention, was inadmissible on the grounds that there had been a deliberate and conscious breach of his constitutional rights. (His right to liberty under Art.40.4.1 of the Constitution.)

The Supreme Court subsequently confirmed this latter decision in *People (DPP) v Lynch* ([1982] I.R. 64). O'Higgins C.J. stated:

> "Once the constitution has been violated for the purposes of securing a confession, the fruits of that violation must be excluded from evidence on that ground alone. Nor can it be said that the matter can safely be left to a decision on fairness or the voluntary nature of the statement."

Unconstitutionally obtained evidence is dealt with in the next chapter. However, a number of issues arise specifically in relation to confession evidence. In particular, two constitutional rights must be considered an individual's right to liberty (Art.40.4.1 of the Constitution) and an individual's right of reasonable access to legal advice (an unenumerated constitutional right).

If the accused's arrest or detention is unlawful then his constitutional right to liberty is breached
Article 40.4.1 of the Constitution provides that "no citizen shall be deprived of his personal liberty save in accordance with law". In general an individual can only be arrested for the purpose of being charged with an offence. The gardaí cannot arrest and detain someone simply to question them, unless they are arrested under a particular statute which gives the gardaí that power. If the gardaí do detain someone for questioning without a statutory power to do so, or if the time limit provided in the statute has expired, the detainee's constitutional right to liberty has been infringed and any confession made is inadmissible. This was clearly established in *Madden*.

Therefore, it is crucial for the gardaí to ensure they are lawfully entitled to arrest and detain someone. The gardaí have been given the power to arrest someone for questioning under a number of statutes. The time limits set out in these statutes will now be considered. There must be strict compliance by the gardaí with the provisions of these statutes.

Under s.30 of the Offences Against The State Act 1939 the gardaí have the power to detain persons on suspicion of having committed a scheduled offence for a period of 24 hours without charge, which may be extended by a further period of 24 hours on the direction of a Chief Superintendent or higher officer. Under s.10 of the Offences Against The State (Amendment) Act 1998 this period may be extended for a further period of 24 hours by order of a district justice. The application must be made by a garda not below the rank of superintendent and he must have reasonable grounds for believing that such further detention is necessary for the proper investigation of the offence concerned. The reasonableness of this suspicion must be proved subsequently at the date of trial or the detention will be deemed to be illegal and any confessions rejected.

The gardaí often used s.30 of the 1939 Act for non-scheduled offences; however, it was felt that this was inappropriate. Therefore, s.4 of the Criminal Justice Act 1984 was introduced. This made provision for a period of detention of an initial period of six hours, followed by a further potential six-hour period if a superintendent has reasonable grounds for believing that such further detention is necessary for the proper investigation of the offence. The offence in question must carry a prison sentence of at least five years' imprisonment.

The Criminal Justice (Drug Trafficking) Act 1996 allows for the prolonged detention of a person arrested without warrant on reasonable suspicion that he has committed a drug trafficking offence. The maximum initial period of detention is six hours, but this may be extended by a further 18 hours if a chief superintendent so directs and has reasonable grounds for so directing. The detention may then be extended by a further 24 hours by further direction of a chief superintendent. Both of these periods require that the chief superintendent have reasonable grounds for believing that such detention is necessary for the proper investigation of the offence. A further extension of up to 72 hours is possible by obtaining a warrant from a District Court or Circuit Court judge. The application must be by a chief superintendent and he must have the same reasonable grounds as before. A final 24-hour period may be obtained by a further application to the judge; again the reasonable grounds are required.

The accused has a constitutional right of reasonable access to a solicitor while in police custody

In *People (DPP) v Healy* ([1990] 2 I.R. 73) the Supreme Court held that reasonable access to legal advice was a constitutional right. Here the accused was arrested under s.30 of the Offences Against the State Act 1939. He was making a confession when a solicitor who had been obtained by his family arrived at the garda station and asked to speak with him. The gardaí did not inform the accused that a solicitor had arrived until after he had finished his statement. The Supreme Court held: "such an important and fundamental standard of fairness in the administration of justice as the right of access to a lawyer must be deemed to be constitutional in its origin". Therefore, they held there had been a breach of the accused's constitutional right which rendered his confession inadmissible. There were no extraordinary excusing circumstances in this case. The court rejected a prosecution argument that telling the accused his solicitor had arrived would have hindered their investigation.

The judgment in *Healy* states that an accused has a right of *reasonable* access to a lawyer. In a number of cases the courts have examined what is meant by the phrase "reasonable access". In *People (DPP) v Buck* ([2002] 2 I.R. 268) the appellant was detained on a Sunday under s.4 of the Criminal Justice Act 1984. The gardaí began to question him at 3.24 p.m. At approximately 5 p.m. the appellant asked to speak to a particular solicitor and said he would not answer any more questions until he had spoken to him. The member in charge of the station tried to get in contact with the solicitor requested. This proved impossible and the appellant requested another solicitor. He could also not be contacted. Eventually at 8.33 p.m. another solicitor arrived to speak with the appellant. While all of this was going on the gardaí continued to question him. The appellant made a confession after he had spoken to the solicitor. The defence claimed that because the accused was denied reasonable access to a solicitor his detention became unconstitutional and, therefore, his subsequent confession was inadmissible. The trial judge held that the confession was admissible as there had not been any mala fides on the part of the gardaí in attempting to get him a solicitor and he did not make the confession until after consulting with a solicitor. The accused was convicted and appealed. The Court of Criminal Appeal upheld this conviction.

However, they certified a point of law of exceptional public importance. The Supreme Court was asked whether the conduct of the gardaí in questioning the accused before he had access to a solicitor but after he had sought access was a deliberate and conscious breach of an accused's constitutional right of access to a solicitor. The Supreme Court said no. They held that the admissibility of a confession made after a solicitor had been requested should be a matter for the trial judge's discretion. The Supreme Court also pointed out that there was no causative link between the alleged breach of the accused's constitutional right of access and his confession as he had spoken to a solicitor before he confessed.

In *Lavery v Member in Charge, Carrickmacross Garda Station* ([1999] 2 I.R. 390) the applicant had been arrested under s.30 of the Offences Against the State Act 1939 on suspicion of belonging to an unlawful organisation. In light of the fact that the Offences Against the State Act 1998 allowed inferences to be drawn from the failure of the accused to answer certain questions put to him, the applicant's solicitor requested that he be present during interviews, that the gardaí record the interview and/or that complete notes be taken and be made available to him. The Supreme Court held that a solicitor is not entitled to be present during interviews, there was no obligation on the gardaí to give a solicitor regular updates as to how an interrogation was progressing and that a solicitor was not entitled to be prescribing the manner in which the interviews would be conducted.

It is worth noting that in *Murray v UK* ((1996) 22 E.H.R.R. 29) the European Court of Human Rights expressed the view that where adverse inferences can be drawn from an accused's decision to remain silent, "it is of paramount importance for the rights of the defence that an accused has access to a lawyer at the initial stages of police interrogation". This issue has not been directly considered in this jurisdiction yet.

An accused does have the right to speak to his solicitor in private. In *People (DPP) v Finnegan* (unreported, July 15, 1997) the appellant was arrested on suspicion of larceny. He asked to speak to his solicitor and was allowed to phone him; the gardaí, however, remained in the room while he made the call. The Court of Criminal Appeal stated that the right to consult a solicitor would usually be of little value unless it carried with it the right to consult him in private.

Controversially, it appears there is no constitutional right for an accused to be informed of his right to a solicitor. This was established in *DPP v Spratt* ([1995] 2 I.L.R.M. 117); otherwise, the court said there would have been no need to list this right in the Criminal Justice Act (Treatment of Persons in Custody in Garda Síochána Stations) Regulations 1987. (These will be dealt with later).

9.4 WAS THERE A BREACH OF THE JUDGES' RULES?

The Judges' Rules are basically a list of directions for the police when dealing with people in custody. They were originally handed down by the judiciary in England in *R v Voisin* ([1918] 1 K.B. 531). In that case Alverston L.C.J. stated: "the rules have not the force of law; they are administrative directions the observance of which police authorities should enforce upon their subordinates as tending to be fair administration of justice." That perspective was accepted by the Irish Supreme Court in *People (AG) v Cummins* ([1972] I.R. 312) which sets out the rules as they apply here:

> "1. When a police officer is endeavouring to discover the author of a crime there is no objection to his putting questions in respect thereof to any person or persons, whether suspected or not, from whom he thinks that useful information may be obtained.
>
> 2. Whenever a police officer has made up his mind to charge a person with a crime, he should first caution such person before asking him any questions, or any further questions as the case may be.
>
> 3. Persons in custody should not be questioned without the usual caution being first administered.
>
> 4. If the prisoner wishes to volunteer any statement, the usual caution should be administered. It is desirable that the last two words of such caution should be omitted, and that the caution should end with the words 'be given in evidence'.
>
> 5. The caution to be administered to a prisoner should therefore be in the following words: 'Do you wish to say anything in answer to the charge? You are not obliged to say anything unless you wish to do so, but whatever you say will be taken down in writing and

may be given in evidence.' Care should be taken to avoid the suggestion that his answers can only be used in evidence *against* him, as this may prevent an innocent person making a statement which might assist to clear him of the charge.

6. A statement made by a prisoner before there is time to caution is not rendered inadmissible in evidence merely because no caution has been given, but in such a case he should be cautioned as soon as possible.

7. A prisoner making a voluntary statement must not be cross-examined, and no question should be put to him about it except for the purpose of removing ambiguity in what he has actually said. For instance, if he has mentioned an hour without saying whether it was morning or evening, or has given a day of the week and day of the month which do not agree, or has not made it clear to what individual or what place he intended to refer in some part of his statement, he may be questioned sufficiently to clear up the point.

8. When two or more persons are charged with the same offence and their statements are taken separately, the police should not read these statements to the other persons charged, but each of such persons should be given by the police a copy of such statements and nothing should be said or done by the police to invite a reply. If the person charged desires to make a statement in reply the usual caution should be administered.

9. Any statement made in accordance with the above rules should, whenever possible, be taken down in writing and signed by the person making it after it has been read to him and he has been invited to make any corrections he may wish."

If one of the Judges' Rules is breached the confession is not automatically inadmissible. Instead, the trial judge has discretion as to whether the confession should be admitted or not. However, in *People (DPP) v Farrell* ([1978] I.R. 13) O'Higgins C.J. stated that although they do not render a confession inadmissible they are "departed from at peril". It should be noted that these rules only apply to confessions.

In *R v Voisin* the accused was charged with murdering a woman. The victim's body was wrapped in paper. The phrase "Bladie Belgiam" was written on the paper. The police questioned the accused and asked him to write the phrase "Bloody Belgian"; he wrote "Bladie Belgiam". It was argued at trial that this evidence was inadmissible, because Rule 4 had been breached, *i.e.* the accused should have been cautioned first. However, the court refused to interfere with the trial judge's discretion to allow the evidence. It was treated as an inculpatory statement.

In *People (AG) v Cummins* ([1972] I.R. 312) the accused was brought into custody on a number of charges. After he was questioned on these charges, the garda asked him about another robbery, saying: "What about Premier Taylor's? I believe you did it". According to Rule 3 if someone is being questioned on another charge they are entitled to another caution. His response was that he had done it and he got £255. The garda then asked him if he wanted to make a statement, to which he replied: "Do you want me to hang myself?" This evidence was admitted and he was convicted. He appealed on the basis, *inter alia*, that this evidence should not have been admissible. In the Supreme Court Walsh J. upheld the admissibility of the statement, saying he would not interfere with the decision of the trial judge who had discretion on this matter.

It is worth noting that a breach of any of the rules may be cured by subsequent compliance with the rule. Therefore, if a successive confession is made after the breach was cured that confession may be admissible. In *People (DPP) v Buckley* ([1990] 1 I.R. 14) the accused was invited to reply to a co-accused's statement in breach of Rule 8. He made a statement. A later attempt was made to rectify the problem, but there was a further breach of the rules (a co-accused was invited into the same room). A further caution was given and a third statement was taken. The Court of Criminal Appeal held that the third confession was admissible despite the inadmissibility of the first two, as the breach of the Judges' Rules had been cured.

9.5 WAS THERE A BREACH OF THE CRIMINAL JUSTICE ACT (TREATMENT OF PERSONS IN CUSTODY IN GARDA SÍOCHÁNA STATIONS) REGULATIONS 1987?

These regulations set out rules which should be followed by the gardaí when they are arresting, detaining or interrogating someone. Section 7(3) of the Criminal Justice Act 1984 provides that:

"A failure on the part of any member of the Garda Síochána to observe any provision of the regulations shall not of it-self… affect the lawfulness of the custody of the detained person or the admissibility in evidence of any statement made by him."

O'Hanlon J. interpreted this section in *DPP v Spratt* ([1995] 2 I.L.R.M. 117). He held that evidence is not automatically inadmissible if the gardaí breach the regulations. Instead the trial judge should decide whether the evidence should be excluded depending on the nature of the breach. In *People (DPP) v McFadden* ([2003] 2 I.R. 105) Keane C.J. suggested that a breach that was not "trivial or inconsequential" should lead to the evidence being held inadmissible. In *People (DPP) v Diver* (unreported, July 29, 2005) Hardiman J. for the Supreme Court held that:

"The issue is not so much whether or not the breach of the regulations was of a *'trivial and inconsequential nature'*, although that is a factor to be taken into account, but whether the fairness of the trial of the accused would be prejudiced by the admission of statements made by him or her in re-spect of which the regulations were not followed."

The following are the most important provisions of the regulations. Article 6 provides that a custody record must be kept for every person who is in custody. This document should record a number of important pieces of information about the person's detention, *e.g.* when they were detained, when they were interviewed and who interviewed them. The member in charge of the garda station should maintain this record. Article 4 defines who this person is. Article 8 provides that the member in charge should inform an arrested person of his right to consult a solicitor.

Article 12 regulates the conduct of interviews. It provides that interviews must be conducted in a fair and humane manner. No more than two gardaí should question an arrested person at any one time and no more than four gardaí should be present during an interview. If an interview has lasted for four hours it should be terminated or adjourned for a reasonable period. The arrested person cannot waive their right to this rest period. Where an arrested person asks to consult a solicitor he should not be asked to make a written statement in relation to an offence until a reasonable time for the attendance of a solicitor has elapsed. Except with the authority of a member in charge an arrested person should not be questioned between midnight and 8 a.m. A member in charge should not give such an authority unless: (1) the arrestee has been taken to the station during that time; or (2) the person is detained under s.4 of the 1984 Act, and has not consented in writing to the suspension of questioning; or (3) the member in charge has reasonable grounds for believing that to delay in questioning would involve a risk of injury to persons, serious loss or damage to property.

Article 12 also requires the gardaí to keep a record of interviews with arrested persons. The Supreme Court considered this provision in *People (DPP) v Diver*. Here the appellant was convicted of murdering his wife on the basis of, *inter alia*, inculpatory statements made while he was in custody. The appellant was interviewed by the gardaí on five occasions. In some of these interviews the gardaí took no notes at all. In others only comments consistent with guilt were recorded while the appellant's persistent denials of the murder charge were not. Hardiman J. described the breaches of the custody regulations as "grave, obvious and deliberate". He said the explanation for the failure to record exculpatory remarks was "incapable of rational belief". There were also problems with other aspects of the prosecution case and, therefore, the accused's conviction was quashed.

In *Diver* Hardiman J. was also critical of the fact that there was no audio-visual recording of the interviews with the accused. He referred to the comments he had previously made in *People (DPP) v Connolly* ([2003] 2 I.R. 1). In that case he stated:

> "The time cannot be remote when we will hear a submission that, absent extraordinary excusing circumstances…it is unacceptable to tender in evidence a statement which has not been so recorded."

Article 13 of the custody regulations concerns minors. It provides that except with the authority of the member in charge, an arrested person who is under 17 shall not be questioned in relation to an offence or asked to make a written statement unless a parent or guardian is present, which authority shall not be given unless: (1) it has not been possible to communicate with a parent or guardian; (2) one has not attended within a reasonable period of time; (3) it is not practical for one to attend within a reasonable period of time; or (4) the member in charge has reasonable grounds for believing that to delay questioning the person would involve a risk to injury to persons or serious loss of or damage to property, destruction of or interference with evidence, or the escape of accomplices. The regulations also provide that where it is reasonable to believe the person is not under 17, the regulations apply as if he were over 17.

9.6 DID THE WAY IN WHICH THE CONFESSION WAS OBTAINED BREACH PRINCIPLES OF FUNDAMENTAL FAIRNESS?

In *People (DPP) v Shaw* ([1982] I.R. 1) Griffin J. stated that even if a confession is technically voluntary it might still be inadmissible if it was obtained in circumstances of unfairness.

The Special Criminal Court applied this principle in *People (DPP) v Ward* (unreported, November 27, 1998). Here the accused was arrested under s.30 of the Offences Against the State Act 1939 for the murder of Veronica Guerin. The court accepted that the accused was "an experienced s.30 detainee" who was well aware of his right to silence and the importance of remaining silent. On the second day of his detention his girlfriend was brought to see him. Neither of them had asked for the meeting. She had also been arrested under s.30 of the 1939 Act and had been detained at a different garda station. She testified that the gardaí told her she could go home if she asked the accused where the gun was and that he could go home if he told them where it was. The prosecution alleged he confessed to certain matters after that meeting. The following day his parents were arrested under s.30 of the 1939 Act as well. When the time for detaining him had nearly expired his mother was rushed to see him although again neither had asked to see the other. This meeting, together with the knowledge that his father had also been arrested, distressed the accused and it was alleged he made a further confession after that. The court held that:

> "Both meetings amounted to a conscious and deliberate disregard of the accused's basic constitutional right to fair procedures and treatment while in custody. They constituted deliberate gross violations of the fundamental obligation which the interrogators and their superiors had of conducting their dealings with the accused in accordance with principles of basic fairness and justice".

Consequently Barr J. held that the accused's alleged confessions were inadmissible.

9.6.1 Confessions and corroboration warnings

Section 10(1) of the Criminal Procedure Act 1993 provides:

> "Where at the trial of a person on indictment evidence is given of a confession made by that person and that evidence is not corroborated, the judge shall advise the jury to have due regard to the absence of corroboration."

The meaning of this provision was considered by the Court of Criminal Appeal in *People (DPP) v Connolly* ([2003] 2 I.R. 1). Here the appellant was convicted solely on the basis of a confession. The trial judge told the jury that that was something they "should bear in mind". The appellant appealed on the basis, *inter alia*, that this direction was insufficient when compared with the words "due regard" in the statute. Hardiman J. in the Court of Appeal accepted this argument, stating that the phrase "bear in mind" is vaguer and less forceful than the statutory phrase. He held that the provision required a trial judge to explain the word corroboration properly to the jury. It was also necessary for the judge to explain to the jury why it is appropriate to look for corroboration. He suggested that the judge could inform the jury that "...there have been a number of instances in the past where admissions have subsequently been proved to be unreliable". Finally, he set out an example of an appropriate corroboration warning. Because of the inadequate direction given to the jury the appellant's conviction was quashed.

10. EVIDENCE OBTAINED IN BREACH OF AN ACCUSED'S CONSTITUTIONAL RIGHTS AND ILLEGALLY OBTAINED EVIDENCE

10.1 Introduction

This chapter will examine two topics: evidence obtained in breach of an accused's constitutional rights and illegally obtained evidence.

10.2 Unconstitutionally obtained evidence

The leading case in this area is the Supreme Court decision in *People (AG) v O'Brien* ([1965] I.R. 142). The two applicants were brothers. During their trial the prosecution introduced into evidence stolen property which had been recovered from their family home. The gardaí had entered that premises on foot of a search warrant. However, there was a mistake on the warrant, which made it invalid. The applicants lived at 118 Captain's Road, Crumlin, but the warrant described it as 118 Cashel Road, Crumlin. The question for the Supreme Court was whether the evidence obtained on foot of this invalid warrant was admissible? In his judgment Walsh J. distinguished between evidence that was obtained illegally and evidence that was obtained in breach of an accused's constitutional right. In this case he held that the court was concerned with a constitutional right, the inviolability of the accused's dwelling, which was protected by Art.40.5 of the Constitution. He held that:

> "The courts in exercising the judicial powers of government of the State must recognise the paramount position of constitutional rights and must uphold the objection of an accused person to the admissibility at his trial of evidence obtained or procured by the State or its servants or agents as a result of a deliberate and conscious violation of the constitutional rights of the accused person where no extraordinary excusing circumstances exist."

In this case the court was satisfied the error on the warrant had been accidental and, therefore, there had been no deliberate and conscious violation of the accused's rights so the evidence was held admissible.

Because the breach was accidental Walsh J. did not expand on what he meant by *a deliberate and conscious* breach of the accused's constitutional rights. After *O'Brien* the exact meaning of this phrase troubled the courts for decades. Two conflicting approaches are evident in the case law. One required that the gardaí actually intended to breach the accused's constitutional right. The other only required the act that caused the breach to be deliberate. Whether the gardaí knew that this act was in breach of the accused's constitutional right was irrelevant because ignorance of the law should never be an excuse.

An example of this latter approach is the Court of Criminal Appeal decision in *People (DPP) v Madden* ([1977] I.R. 336). Here the applicant had been detained for questioning under s.30 of The Offences Against The State Act 1939. His detention continued beyond the time limit allowed in the Act. The Court of Criminal Appeal held that:

> "[w]hat was done or permitted...may have been done or permitted for the best of motives and in the interests of the due investigation of the crime. However, it was done or permitted without regard to the right to liberty guaranteed to this defendant by Article 40 of the Constitution."

Therefore, the evidence obtained was ruled inadmissible.

The Supreme Court also considered this issue in *People (DPP) v Shaw* ([1982] I.R. 1). In contrast to *Madden*, here Griffin J. for the majority held: "In my opinion, it is the violation of the person's constitutional rights, and not the particular act complained of, that has to be deliberate and conscious for the purpose of ruling out the statement." Walsh J. dissented, holding that it "is the doing of the act which is the essential matter, not the actor's appreciation of the legal consequences or incidents of it".

The Supreme Court finally resolved this issue in *People (DPP) v Kenny* ([1990] I.L.R.M. 569). Here the appellant's flat had been under surveillance by the gardaí. They observed suspicious behaviour and obtained a search warrant under s.26 of the Misuse of Drugs Act 1977. On foot of this warrant the gardaí forced their way into the flat and found a quantity of drugs. This was the only evidence against the appellant. He was convicted. The Court of Criminal Appeal held that the procedure used to obtain the search warrant rendered it invalid but they nonetheless upheld his conviction. The question for the Supreme Court was whether the forcible entry into the appellant's home by the gardaí on foot of this invalid search warrant was a deliberate and conscious violation of the accused's rights so as to render the evidence obtained inadmissible. Finlay C.J. gave the judgment for the majority. He recognised the divergent approaches in the previous case law and concluded that he could not follow the decision of the majority of the Supreme Court in *Shaw*. Instead he felt the court had an obligation to choose the principle which would vindicate the constitutional rights of the citizen most effectively. He stated:

> "To exclude only evidence obtained by a person who knows or ought reasonably to know that he is invading a constitutional right is to impose a negative deterrent...
> To apply, on the other hand, the absolute protection rule of exclusion whilst providing also that negative deterrent, incorporates as well a positive encouragement to those in authority over the crime preventions and detection services of the State to consider in detail the personal rights of the citizens as set out in the Constitution, and the effect of their powers of arrest, detention, search and questioning in relation to such rights".

Therefore, the accused's conviction was quashed. Griffin J. dissented. He repeated the view he had expressed in *Shaw*.

Consequently, for evidence to be excluded there must be:

(a) a breach of an accused's constitutional rights;
(b) a causative link between that breach and the evidence obtained; and
(c) no extraordinary excusing circumstances.

10.2.1 Breach of an accused's constitutional rights

This requirement has been interpreted in quite an unusual way. The leading decision on this issue is Griffin J.'s judgment in *Shaw*. Here the appellant and another man were arrested by the gardaí for being in possession of a stolen car. However, the gardaí also suspected that the men were responsible for the disappearance of two women. The gardaí were concerned for the safety of these women so they did not bring the two men before the District Court at the first reasonable opportunity. Instead they were kept in custody for several days and were interrogated as to the whereabouts of the women. Eventually both men made confessions in relation to the women.

The trial judge held these confessions were admissible in evidence. The appellant claimed his confession was obtained in breach of his constitutional right to liberty and so should have been inadmissible.

In the Supreme Court Griffin J. for the majority accepted that prima facie the appellant's detention was unlawful. However, he held that no one has an absolute right to liberty. Here the State also had an obligation to vindicate a competing constitutional right, the women's right to life. In such circumstances the State must protect the more important right. In this case the women's right to life outweighed the appellant's right to liberty. Therefore, in continuing the appellant's detention, the gardaí were not acting unlawfully but were doing what was necessary to protect the constitutional rights of the women. Walsh J. dissented, he believed the appellant's constitutional right to liberty had been breached; however, he held the confession was admissible because there were extraordinary excusing circumstances.

The Supreme Court considered this issue again in *DPP v Delaney* ([1997] 3 I.R. 453) and approved the majority judgment in *Shaw*. A crowd gathered outside a flat and were threatening to burn it down when the gardaí arrived. The five appellants (which included the owner of the flat) had barricaded themselves in the flat and were armed with weapons. The gardaí were told there were children in the flat so they decided to forcibly enter the flat. Four children were recovered unharmed. The five appellants were arrested and charged with various offences. The appellants claimed that the gardaí had entered the flat illegally and in breach of the owner's constitutional right to the inviolability of his dwelling. O'Flaherty J. gave the Supreme Court judgment. He noted that *Shaw* decided that there was a hierarchy of constitutional rights and when conflict arises between them that which ranks higher must prevail. He concluded that:

> "The sergeant was entitled to enter the premises to safe-guard the life and limb of the woman who was there as well as the children…He was entitled to make the choice that he did and such choice, far from being in breach of the Constitution, was in fulfilment of the obligation that devolves on all citizens to observe and implement the requirements of the Constitution because the safeguarding of life and limb must be more important than the inviolability of the dwelling of a citizen, especially when it is under attack in any event."

10.2.2 A causative link between the breach and the evidence obtained

The evidence sought to be excluded must have been obtained as a result of the breach of the accused's constitutional rights. This requirement was considered in *Walsh v District Justice O'Buachalla* ([1991] 1 I.R. 56). Here the applicant had been convicted of drunk driving contrary to s.49 of the Road Traffic Act 1961. He was brought to a garda station where he had to wait for a doctor to arrive to take a sample. It took about 40 minutes before the doctor saw him and while he was waiting he was given a document which informed him of his right to consult with a solicitor. He did not ask for a solicitor until the doctor was just about to take the sample from him. Thinking this was simply a delaying tactic the garda refused to let him contact a solicitor at that point and the sample was taken. He was convicted. He sought to have his conviction quashed on the basis that the garda's refusal was in breach of his constitutional right of access to a solicitor. Blayney J. rejected this application. He held that even if there was a breach of the accused's constitutional rights, which he doubted, there was no causal link between the breach and the evidence obtained. The applicant was obliged by statute to give a specimen of blood or urine and no advice from a solicitor could have altered that position. Therefore, his being refused access to a solicitor did not in any way lead to the specimen of blood being obtained.

10.2.3 No extraordinary excusing circumstances

If evidence is obtained in breach of an accused's constitutional right it may still be admitted if there are extraordinary excusing circumstances in the case. The prosecution bear the burden of proving the existence of such circumstances. In *O'Brien*, Walsh J. set out three examples of extraordinary excusing circumstances. They were: (a) "the imminent destruction of vital evidence"; (b) "the need to rescue a victim in peril"; and (c) "evidence obtained by a search incidental to and contemporaneous with a lawful arrest although made without a valid search warrant". Since the decision in *Shaw* it is arguable that the second example is no longer valid. If a victim is in peril then presumably their constitutional right to life would trump whatever constitutional right of the accused is at issue.

A good example of extraordinary excusing circumstances is the decision of Carney J. in *Freeman v DPP* ([1996] 3 I.R. 565). Here the appellant and two other men were unloading goods from a van and carrying them into his house. The men saw some gardaí approaching, so they ran into the house and slammed the door. The gardaí forcibly entered the house without waiting for a warrant. They discovered various stolen goods inside. Carney J. accepted that the gardaí had entered the house in breach of the appellant's constitutional right to the inviolability of his dwelling. However, he held the evidence was admissible because there were extraordinary excusing circumstances. The men had been caught in *flagrante delicto* and the goods would have been destroyed by the time a warrant could have been obtained.

10.3 EVIDENCE OBTAINED ILLEGALLY (BUT NOT UNCONSTITUTIONALLY)

People (AG) v O'Brien is also the leading authority on illegally obtained evidence. The majority of the Supreme Court held that a trial judge has a discretion whether to admit such evidence or not. In exercising this discretion Kingsmill Moore J. held that the trial judge should look at all the circumstances of the case. He then detailed a number of factors that the trial judge should have regard to:

> "Was the illegal action intentional or unintentional, and, if intentional, was it the result of an *ad hoc* decision or does it represent a settled or deliberate policy? Was the illegality one of a trivial and technical nature or was it a serious invasion of important rights the recurrence of which would involve a real danger to necessary freedoms? Were there circumstances of urgency or emergency which provide some excuse for the action?"

10.4 EXAMPLES OF CONSTITUTIONAL RIGHTS THAT MAY BE BREACHED

So far this chapter has considered the principles to be applied when evidence is obtained unconstitutionally and illegally. It will now examine how these principles have been applied in practice. There are a number of constitutional rights that an accused person might seek to rely on to exclude evidence. In the last chapter the two constitutional rights most commonly relied on to exclude confessions were considered. A similar approach will be adopted here. The constitutional rights that will be considered are the inviolability of the dwelling and an accused's right to liberty.

10.4.1 The inviolability of the dwelling

Article 40.5 of the Constitution provides that the dwelling of every citizen is inviolable and shall not be forcibly entered save in accordance with law. It is clear from the wording of this provision that the gardaí will not breach it if they have a lawful authority for entering the dwelling. Such authority may be provided by the consent of the owner, by a valid search warrant, or by statute. Each of these options will now be considered.

If the owner of a dwelling expressly consents to garda entry then no breach of his constitutional right occurs. The courts have also been prepared to imply consent in certain circumstances. In *People (DPP) v Forbes* ([1994] 2 I.R. 542) the accused was arrested on the forecourt of another person's premises. There was no evidence that the owner had withdrawn his consent to the gardaí. In *obiter dicta* it appears the Supreme Court was prepared to accept that the gardaí have the implied consent of a householder to enter onto his premises to prevent a breach of the law.

In *People (DPP) v McCann* ([1998] 4 I.R. 397) the appellant was convicted of the murder of his wife and child. They had died in a fire in their family home, which was attached to a pub run by the family. The gardaí obtained forensic evidence from the burnt-out dwelling. One of the appellant's grounds of appeal was that this evidence was obtained in breach of his constitutional right to the inviolability of his dwelling. The Court of Criminal Appeal held that as the appellant had requested the gardaí to investigate the offence he had impliedly consented to their presence on the premises.

The position in relation to search warrants is straightforward. The gardaí may enter premises on foot of a valid search warrant. However, if the warrant is invalid, *Kenny* makes clear that any evidence obtained is inadmissible.

However, the gardaí may not necessarily need a warrant. Several statutes authorise them to enter premises without one. Section 6(2) of the Criminal Law Act 1997 provides that for the purpose of arresting someone for an arrestable offence a garda can enter (if necessary by using reasonable force) any premises (including a dwelling) where the person is or where the garda suspects them to be. However, if the premises is a dwelling, a garda may only enter when he observes the suspect entering the dwelling; or the suspect ordinarily resides at that dwelling; or he suspects that before a warrant could be obtained, the person will either abscond for the purposes of avoiding justice, or will obstruct the course of justice, or will commit an arrestable offence. The Road Traffic Act 1994 also allows the gardaí to enter a dwelling without a warrant. They may do so to arrest a driver believed to have caused injury if they observe the driver entering the dwelling.

The other issue that needs to be examined is what exactly a dwelling is. In some situations it will be obvious that the premises entered was a dwelling. In *Jeffrey v Black* ((1978) 1 All E.R. 555) the accused was arrested for stealing a sandwich from a pub. Before he was taken to the police station he was brought home and his room was searched without his consent. There the police found cannabis. This evidence was held to be inadmissible by the Court of Appeal.

However, in other situations it will be less clear-cut. In *Forbes* the Supreme Court held that the forecourt of a house was not a dwelling. In *DPP v McMahon* ([1986] I.R. 393) the owners of licensed premises were charged with offences contrary to the Gaming and Lotteries Act 1956. The gardaí had obtained evidence by entering the premises without a search warrant and without identifying themselves as gardaí. The Supreme Court accepted that the gardaí could not rely on the owners' implied invitation to the public and were therefore trespassers. However, they held that a licensed premises is not a dwelling. Therefore, no breach of the owner's constitutional rights occurred. Instead, the entry of the gardaí was illegal and the trial judge had a discretion to admit the evidence. This would suggest that any business premises should not be regarded as a dwelling for the purposes of Art.40.5 of the Constitution unless the accused also lives there.

10.4.2 An accused's right to liberty

Article 40.4.1 of the Constitution provides that no citizen shall be deprived of his liberty save in accordance with law. This provision was considered in the last chapter in relation to confession evidence; however, it is also possible for the gardaí to obtain other types of evidence in breach of an accused's right to liberty. The statutory periods limiting the length of time for which an arrested person can be detained are equally applicable here.

A good example of non-confession evidence obtained in breach of an accused's constitutional right to liberty is the Supreme Court decision in *DPP v Finn* ([2003] 1 I.R. 372). Here the appellant was arrested on suspicion of drunk driving contrary to s.49(8) of the Road Traffic Act 1961. He was brought to a garda station where he was kept under observation for approximately 20 minutes. He was then asked to provide two specimens of his breath. The reason given for the observation period was that in guidelines given to gardaí an arrested person should be observed for 20 minutes prior to giving a sample to ensure the person does not consume any food, which could make the test result inaccurate.

The question for the Supreme Court was whether this 20-minute observation period rendered the appellant's detention unlawful. The appellant relied on two previous cases, *Dunne v Clinton* ([1930] I.R. 366) and *People v Walsh* ([1980] I.R. 303). In the latter case the Supreme Court held that once an accused is arrested and detained, "[t]he important thing is that his detention after arrest must only be for the purpose of bringing him before a District Justice or a Peace Commissioner with reasonable expedition." Here the court noted that the appellant was not arrested for the purpose of being brought before a court. He was arrested and detained for a purpose authorised by statute, *i.e.* the taking of specimens of his breath. In view of the decision in *Walsh* the Supreme Court felt that the arresting gardaí were under a duty to require the appellant to provide his specimens with reasonable expedition. Here the Supreme Court did not regard the length of the delay as significant. Instead they were more concerned with the fact that this extra period of detention seemed to be a pre-established practice on the part of the gardaí. They felt there was an onus on the prosecution to justify this practice and they held that the prosecution had failed to do that here. Therefore, the evidence obtained was inadmissible.

Another issue that has arisen in this area is whether an accused can be lawfully arrested for one offence and questioned about other offences or if this is a breach of his constitutional right to liberty. The Supreme Court considered this question in *People (DPP) v Quilligan and O'Reilly (No.3)* ([1987] I.L.R.M. 606). Here the accused was detained under s.30 of the Offences Against the State Act 1939 for questioning on the scheduled offence of causing malicious damage to a house. However, the gardaí also wanted to question him about a murder, which is not in the schedule of the 1939 Act. The Supreme

Court held that this procedure was lawful once it could be established that the arresting garda had suspicion that the accused had also been involved in the scheduled offence and that his arrest was genuinely for the purpose of investigating the scheduled offence even if he was questioned about another offence.

This decision was approved in *People (DPP) v Howley* ([1989] I.L.R.M. 629). Here the appellant was also arrested under s.30 of the 1939 Act and questioned about a murder. In this case the scheduled offence was cattle-maiming. The appellant claimed that the scheduled offence should be the predominant reason for the arrest or else it should be ruled unlawful. The Supreme Court rejected this. They held the practice was valid once there was a genuine desire on the part of the gardaí to pursue the investigation of the scheduled offence.

11. EXPERT AND OPINION EVIDENCE

11.1 INTRODUCTION

There is a general rule of evidence that witnesses can only testify about facts. They are not allowed to express opinions or draw inferences from facts. This is because as Kingsmill Moore J. put it in *AG (Ruddy) v Kenny* ((1960) 94 I.L.T.R. 185): "It is for the tribunal of fact judge or jury as the case may be to draw inferences of fact, form opinions and come to conclusions." If a witness were to do so he would be usurping the function of the judge or jury.

However, like many other general rules of law this rule has its exceptions. First, there is an exception that permits expert witnesses to give opinion evidence, *e.g.* a doctor in a medical negligence action. Secondly, non-experts can give opinion evidence in certain circumstances. Frequently this evidence is admitted, as the facts would not make much sense without the opinion, *e.g.* a witness may give an opinion as to how fast a car was travelling.

This chapter will examine these two exceptions.

11.2 EXPERT EVIDENCE

11.2.1 When is a witness considered to be an expert?

While it is common for one side to challenge the testimony of the other side's expert, it is rare for their expertise to be disputed. Therefore, this issue has not been directly considered in courts in this jurisdiction very often. In *AG (Ruddy) v Kenny* Kingsmill Moore J. stated:

> "the tribunal may be assisted by the evidence of persons qualified by experience, training and knowledge, to guide the tribunal to the correct conclusions. Such persons, generally described as experts, may express their opinions."

Therefore, it would appear that in considering this issue a court would look for experience, training and knowledge. However, it is clear from the decision in *R v Silverlock* ([1894] 2 Q.B. 766) that formal qualifications are not essential as the court permitted a solicitor who had a bit of an interest in handwriting to give expert testimony.

11.2.2 Rationale

The rationale for this exception is fairly obvious. Experts by definition are specialists in their chosen field. They are allowed give opinion evidence or draw inferences in their area of specialisation because judges or juries would not have the knowledge required to do so. As Kingsmill Moore J. put it in *AG (Ruddy) v Kenny*:

> "The nature of the issue may be such that even if the tribunal of fact had been able to make the observations in person he or they would not have been possessed of the experience or the specialised knowledge necessary to observe the significant facts, or to evaluate the matters observed and to draw the correct inferences of fact."

For example, in a medical negligence action a judge may need to be advised by a medical expert of the procedures the defendant should or should not have done. Without this information the judge would not be in a position to assess if the defendant was negligent or not.

11.2.3 The limits on the admissibility of expert evidence

This rationale also limits the matters upon which an expert can state his opinion. Obviously he should only testify on matters that he is an expert in. Furthermore, if the matter is something that does not require the testimony of an expert then expert evidence is inadmissible. The reason for this is that there is a danger that a jury may give too much weight to an expert's opinion. In *R v Turner* ((1975) 61 Cr. App. R. 67) Lawton L.J. stated:

> "If on the proven facts a judge or jury can form their own conclusions without help, then the opinion of an expert is unnecessary. In such a case if it is given up in scientific jargon it may make judgment more difficult. The fact that an expert witness has impressive scientific qualifications does not by that fact alone make his opinion on matters of human nature and behaviour within the limits of normality any more helpful than that of the jurors themselves; but there is a danger that they may think it does."

So, for example, if I slip on a wet floor in a supermarket I cannot have an expert testify that I was more likely to slip on the floor because it was wet. That fact is something that a judge would already know.

A question then arises as to where to draw the line between situations where the testimony of an expert is required and cases where it is unnecessary. This issue has come before the courts on a number of occasions, particularly in criminal cases where the accused's state of mind is in issue. Obviously expert medical evidence is admissible if the accused is relying on the defence of insanity, automatism or otherwise claiming that he lacks the capacity to form the requisite *mens rea*. For example, in *R v Toner* ((1991) 93 Cr. App. R. 382) the accused was charged with attempted murder. A doctor was permitted to give evidence that the accused suffered a mild hypoglycaemic attack (a low blood sugar condition), which may have prevented him from forming the required intention to kill.

However, the courts have not allowed defendants to rely on expert evidence to show that they were really upset on the day in question, or that their victim provoked them, because these are issues that judges and juries are competent to decide for themselves without the help of experts.

In *R v Turner* the accused killed his girlfriend by hitting her repeatedly on the head with a hammer. He was charged with murder. He tried to rely on the defence of provocation. He stated he was deeply in love with her and that he thought she was pregnant with his child. On the night she was killed he claimed she told him with a grin on her face that she had been sleeping with other men and that the child was not his. He stated that this made him very upset, that he lost control and reached for the hammer. The defence sought to call a psychiatrist to give evidence that the accused "had a deep emotional relationship with the girl which was likely to have caused an explosive release of blind rage when she confessed her wantonness to him". The trial judge held that the evidence of the psychiatrist was inadmissible. The Court of Appeal affirmed this ruling. Lawdon L. J. gave the judgment of the court:

> "We all know that both men and women who are deeply in love can, and sometimes do, have outbursts of blind rage when discovering unexpected wantonness on the part of their loved ones...Jurors do not need psychiatrists to tell them how ordinary folk who are not suffering from any mental illness are likely to react to the stresses and strains of life. It follows that the proposed evidence was not admissible to establish that the appellant was likely to have been provoked."

The Court of Criminal Appeal approved the decision in *Turner* in *People (DPP) v Kehoe* ([1992] I.L.R.M. 481). The applicant was convicted of murder and sought leave to appeal. The facts of the case were not in dispute. The applicant had a relationship with a woman with whom he had a child. The woman then started seeing the deceased who up to that point had been the applicant's best friend. On the night in question the applicant and the woman went for a few drinks together and then went back to her apartment. The applicant decided to look in on his son. When he went into what he thought was his son's room he found his former best friend asleep. The applicant gave evidence that this shocked and upset him. He went into the kitchen, got a knife, ran back to the room and stabbed the deceased. The applicant sought to rely on the defence of provocation. To support this contention a psychiatrist gave evidence on his behalf. The applicant sought leave to appeal on the basis that the trial judge had misdirected the jury in relation to the psychiatrist's evidence. The Court of Criminal Appeal began by noting that the only defence put forward was provocation rather than any form of mental illness and that the psychiatrist attempted to reinforce this defence by expanding on the accused's testimony that he had been upset. They then stated:

> "The court is of the opinion that the accused's defence was properly to be considered by the jury without such elaboration and that, further, in the course of his evidence, it is clear that Dr. Behan overstepped the mark in saying that he believed the accused did not have an intention to kill and that the accused was telling the truth. These are clearly matters four-square within the jury's function and a witness, no more than the trial judge or anyone else is not entitled to trespass on what is the jury's function."

One rather controversial case on this issue is the decision in *Lowery v R* ([1974] A.C. 85). Here Lowery and another man, King, were tried for the vicious murder of a young girl. Lowery was convicted. During the trial the judge admitted evidence of a psychologist on behalf of King. He testified that of the two accused, Lowery had the personality more disposed towards the commission of the acts in question. The Privy Council upheld the admissibility of this evidence. However, the court in *Turner* stressed that this case should be limited to its own special facts.

11.2.4 Expert evidence and the ultimate issue rule

There was a traditional rule at common law that prohibited expert witnesses giving their opinion or drawing inferences in respect of the ultimate issue in the case because as noted above this would usurp the function of the judge or jury. Having said that, in relation to experts the rule is somewhat absurd as the whole basis for admitting such evidence is that the judge or jury do not have sufficient knowledge to draw their own inferences. It is therefore no surprise that the rule has gone into decline in recent years. But it is still ultimately up to the judge or jury to make the decision in the case they are hearing. A good example of this is *People (AG) v Fennell* (No.1) ([1940] I.R. 445). Here the Court of Criminal Appeal refused to overturn a jury finding that the accused was guilty in circumstances where two medical experts had testified that he was insane at the time of the killing.

11.2.5 The weight to be given to expert evidence

The weight that a judge or jury gives to an expert's evidence will depend on a number of factors including the particular circumstances of the case, the experience of the expert and the type of evidence tendered. There is a danger that judges and/or juries will attach too much weight to expert evidence. This is particularly so when the evidence in question is a recent scientific development whose limitations have not been established. A famous example of this is *R v McIlkenny* ((1991) 93 Cr. App. R. 287) which is better known as the *Birmingham Six Case*. In that case the prosecution relied on the Greiss test to prove that the defendants when arrested had recently been in contact with explosives. Their experts said the result was 99 per cent certain. The trial judge described this evidence as the clearest and most overwhelming evidence he had ever heard. However, by the time the Court of Appeal heard the case the certainty of this test result had been totally undermined. The use of playing cards by some of the defendants could also have produced a positive test result.

Similarly there is a risk that judges and/or juries could trust DNA evidence too much. This danger was highlighted in *People (DPP) v Allen* ([2003] 4 I.R. 295) in the Court of Criminal Appeal. Here McCracken J. stated:

"Expert evidence comparing D.N.A. profiles is a comparatively recent scientific technique and indeed it would appear that it is still being perfected. As in many scientific advances, the jury have to rely on expert evidence. One of the primary dangers involved in such circumstances is that, the matter being so technical, a jury could jump to the conclusion that the evidence is infallible. That, of course, is not so in the case of D.N.A. evidence, at least in the present state of knowledge."

An example of this infallibility is the decision in *R v Pitchfork* (*The Guardian*, January 23, 1988). Here the accused was convicted of murder. However, he initially avoided being arrested by substituting a friend's sample for his own.

11.2.6 The duties of the expert witness

As noted earlier the reason why the opinions of expert witnesses are admissible is that judges and/or juries do not have the knowledge they need. In other words the experts are there to assist the court in making an informed decision. This places a duty on the experts. They should not simply represent their client's interest, but instead they should fairly and objectively give the court the knowledge it needs to come to a just conclusion. Unfortunately this does not always happen and frequently experts are guilty of favouring the side that called them. In *Abbey Mortgages Plc v Key Surveyors Nationwide Ltd* ([1996] 1 W.L.R. 1534) the Court of Appeal noted:

"For whatever reason, and whether consciously or unconsciously, the fact is that expert witnesses instructed on behalf of parties to litigation often tend, if called as witnesses at all, to expouse [*sic*] the cause of those instructing them to a greater or lesser extent, on occasion becoming more partisan than the parties."

Because of this tendency Cresswell J. in *National Justice Compania Naviera S.A. v Prudential Assurance Co. Ltd ("The Ikarian Reefer")* ([1993] 2 Lloyd's Rep. 68) felt it appropriate to set out the following guidelines for expert witnesses:

"1. Expert evidence presented to the Court should be, and should be seen to be, the independent product of the expert uninfluenced as to form or content by the exigencies of litigation.

2. An expert witness should provide independent assistance to the Court by way of objective unbiased opinion in relation to matters within his expertise.

3. An expert witness should state the facts or assumption upon which his opinion is based. He should not omit to consider material facts which could detract from his concluded opinion.

4. An expert witness should make it clear when a particular question or issue falls outside his expertise.

5. If an expert's opinion is not properly researched because he considers that insufficient data is available, then this must be stated with an indication that the opinion is no more than a provisional one.

6. If, after exchange of reports, an expert witness changes his view on a material matter having read the other side's report or for any other reason, such change of view should be communicated ... to the other side".

11.3 Non-Expert Opinion Evidence

In general non-expert witnesses can give their opinion when it is intertwined with facts they are recounting so it would be virtually impossible to separate the facts from the opinion, or where it would not make any sense to state the facts without the opinion. It would be almost impossible to set out an exhaustive list of the specific situations where non-experts are permitted to do this. As Lavery J. in *AG (Ruddy) v Kenny* stated: "There are innumerable incidents of everyday life upon which an ordinary person can express a useful opinion and one which ought to be admitted."

The reality is that almost every time a witness testifies he or she expresses an opinion. If a witness states that the person they saw was old, surely that is an opinion rather than an objective fact. A child witness could describe a man in his thirties as old while a 70-year-old could say they were young (personally I prefer the latter view). It is up to the party cross-examining the witness to try and establish what the witness means by old or why the witness thinks the person is old.

One question that has come before the courts is whether a non-expert can testify about whether an accused was drunk or not. In *R v Davies* ([1962] 1 W.L.R. 1111) the accused was charged with driving a car when "unfit to drive through drink". At his trial a witness testified that the accused was under the influence of drink and was in no condition to drive. On appeal the court held that a non-expert witness could give his impression as to whether drink had been taken or not. However, he could not give his opinion as to fitness to drive, as that was the ultimate issue for the court to determine.

The issue was considered in this jurisdiction in *AG (Ruddy) v Kenny*. The defendant was being prosecuted before the District Court for a drink driving offence. A garda was giving evidence and was about to be asked if he thought the accused was drunk when the solicitor for the accused objected. The district judge stated a case to the High Court. The question asked was whether the evidence of a garda that the defendant was unfit to drive because he was drunk was admissible. In the High Court Davitt P. held:

> "Drunkenness, unfortunately, is a condition which is not so exceptional or so much outside the experience of the ordinary individual that it should require an expert to diagnose it. In my opinion a Garda witness, or an ordinary witness, may give evidence of his opinion as to whether a person is drunk or not."

He also said that a non-expert may express his opinion as to whether a defendant is drunk to such an extent as to be incapable of exercising proper control of a car. The majority of the Supreme Court upheld this decision. Kingsmill Moore J. dissented and stated:

> "It is a longstanding rule of our law of evidence that with certain exceptions a witness may not express an opinion as to a fact in issue. Ideally, in the theory of our law, a witness may testify only to the existence of fact, which he has observed with one or more of his five senses. It is for the tribunal of fact, judge or jury as the case may be, to draw inferences of fact, form opinions and come to conclusions."

The law in this jurisdiction has now been changed. One's capacity to drive is no longer relevant. Instead, prosecutions are based on the concentration of alcohol in the blood or urine.

Section 21 of the Offences Against the State Act 1939 makes it an offence to be a member of certain unlawful organisations. Section 3(2) of the Offences Against the State (Amendment) Act 1972 provides, for the purposes of a charge under s.21 of the 1939 Act, that where a garda, not below the rank of chief superintendent, states his belief that the accused was at a material time a member of an unlawful organisation, the statement shall be evidence that he was such a member.

The constitutionality of this latter provision was challenged in *AG v O'Leary* ([1991] I.L.R.M. 454). Costello J. rejected an argument that as this provision rendered the garda's evidence conclusive of the fact of membership it was contrary to the presumption of innocence. Instead, he held that all the section did was render admissible the non-expert opinion evidence of the garda "which would otherwise be inadmissible."

12. PRIVILEGE

12.1 INTRODUCTION

Privilege is a right enjoyed by a person or a body which entitles them to refuse to produce a document or to answer a question. For example, a witness does not have to answer any question that would incriminate him. Privilege can be divided into a number of categories:

1) legal professional privilege;
2) without prejudice communications;
3) privilege against self-incrimination;
4) journalistic privilege;
5) informer privilege;
6) marital privilege;
7) sacerdotal privilege;
8) public interest privilege.

Each of these categories will be considered in turn.

12.2 LEGAL PROFESSIONAL PRIVILEGE

According to Kelly J. in *Miley v Flood* ([2001] 2 I.R. 50), "[l]egal professional privilege is more than a mere rule of evidence. It is a fundamental condition on which the administration of justice as a whole rests." The reason why legal professional privilege is so important is as follows: A client must be sure that what he tells his lawyer in confidence cannot be revealed to anyone else. Otherwise he might not tell his lawyer the full story and consequently his lawyer would not be able to advise him properly. This would not be in the interests of justice. However, it also has to be recognised that this rule has its drawbacks. As the Supreme Court pointed out in *Gallagher v Stanley and National Maternity Hospital* ([1998] 2 I.R. 267), "[i]n general, justice will be best served where there is the greatest candour and where all relevant documentary evidence is available." The Supreme Court then went on to recognise this contradiction: "Both principles, full disclosure on the one hand and legal professional privilege on the other, are there to advance the cause of justice. Sometimes they may be on a collision course." Therefore, limits have to be placed on this doctrine. The courts have recognised two sub-categories of legal professional privilege, legal advice privilege and litigation privilege.

12.2.1 Legal advice privilege

Communications between a lawyer and a client for the purpose of giving or receiving legal advice are privileged. Therefore, such communications do not have to be disclosed. For a document or a piece of information to be covered by legal advice privilege it must satisfy a number of requirements.

12.2.1.1 There must be a communication

Communication is given a wide interpretation. It covers both written and oral communications. It also would include any notes made by the lawyer of conversations with the client. However, it is important to note that only communications between a lawyer and a client are covered here. Communications by the lawyer or the client with third parties are not protected even if these are necessary to obtain the legal advice.

12.2.1.2 The communication must be confidential

Legal advice privilege only attaches to communications which are intended to be confidential. This requirement was considered in *Bord na gCon v Murphy* ([1970] I.R. 301). Here the defendant was convicted of breaches of the Greyhound Industry Act 1958 and appealed. The complainant had written to the defendant accusing him of contravening the Act and asked him to furnish them with any observations he wished to make. The defendant made a statement to his solicitor setting out his side of the story and the solicitor then wrote back to the board enclosing a written note of the statement. The complainants wanted to rely on the letter and statement in the Supreme Court. The Supreme Court held that they were inadmissible as hearsay. However, they also held that the documents were not privileged because it was not intended that the contents would remain confidential. Rather it was intended that the contents would be disclosed to the board.

12.2.1.3 The communication must be made in the course of a professional legal relationship

The communication must be made to or by the lawyer in the course of a professional legal relationship or with the intention of establishing one. In *Buckley v Incorporated Law Society* ([1994] 2 I.R. 44) the defendants tried to claim privilege over letters of complaint they had received from the clients of a particular solicitor. This claim was rejected, as the complainants were not consulting the defendant as a legal adviser.

12.2.1.4 The communication must be for the purpose of obtaining legal advice

Communications between a lawyer and a client are only privileged if they are for the purpose of giving or receiving legal advice. So if my solicitor decides to send me a Christmas card I cannot claim privilege over it. In other words, a distinction can be drawn between communications for legal advice (which are privileged) and communications for other purposes (which are not privileged). The Supreme Court highlighted this distinction in *Smurfit Paribas Bank Ltd v A.A.B. Export Finance Ltd* ([1990] 1 I.R. 469). Here the plaintiff and the defendant both lent money to the same third party in separate transactions and the third party agreed to create charges over his assets to secure the money lent. The plaintiff sought discovery of correspondence and instructions passing between the defendant and the solicitors that acted for them when the charge was created. The defendant claimed these documents were privileged. This claim was rejected by the High Court, as the documents did not contain any legal advice. In the Supreme Court Finlay C.J. began by looking at the underlying rationale of why privilege attaches to lawyer/client communications. He noted that it enabled a client to tell his lawyer the full story so the lawyer could advise him properly. This he accepted was important for the proper administration of justice. However, he also noted that the rule had disadvantages. It reduces disclosure, which makes it harder for a court to discover the truth. Therefore he held that privilege should:

> "only be granted by the courts in instances which have been identified as securing an objective which in the public interest in the proper conduct of the administration of justice can be said to outweigh the disadvantage arising from the restriction of disclosure of all the relevant facts."

He felt that this only happened when the communication is closely and proximately linked to the conduct of litigation and the function of the administration of justice. He held that legal advice came within this requirement. He then stated:

> "Similar considerations do not, however, it seems to me, apply to communications made to a lawyer for the purpose of obtaining his legal assistance other than advice. There are many tasks carried out by a lawyer for his client, other

than the giving of advice, which could not be said to contain any real relationship with the area of potential litigation. For such communications there does not appear to me to be any sufficient public interest to be secured, which could justify an exemption from disclosure."

Kelly J. acknowledged this distinction between legal advice and legal assistance in *Miley v Flood* ([2001] 2 I.R. 50). Here the Flood Tribunal ordered the applicant to furnish it with the name of his client. The applicant claimed that the identity of his client was covered by legal professional privilege. Kelly J. rejected this argument. He held that a client's identity was a collateral fact, which had nothing to do with the giving or receiving of legal advice.

It has to be noted that in *Gallagher v Stanley*, the Supreme Court commented that legal professional privilege "attaches to confidential communications passing between lawyer and client for the purpose of obtaining legal advice or assistance". This case was actually concerned with litigation privilege so this comment should not be taken as overturning the *Smurfit Paribas Bank Ltd* decision. Instead, this comment merely serves to highlight the fact that it is difficult to say what the difference between legal advice and legal assistance is. Therefore, the important issue from *Smurfit Paribas Bank Ltd* would appear to be whether the task contains "any real relationship with the area of potential litigation". The fact that the court described communications which satisfied this test as legal advice is a secondary consideration.

12.2.2 Litigation privilege

The second category of legal professional privilege is litigation privilege. Once again there has to be a communication; however, here the communication can be between the lawyer or client and a third party. As with legal advice privilege a number of requirements have to be met.

12.2.2.1 Litigation must be pending or contemplated
To come within this category the litigation must be pending or contemplated. This requirement has been considered in a number of cases. In *Kerry County Council v Liverpool Salvage Association* ((1903) 38 I.L.T.R. 7) the claim of privilege failed because no litigation had been contemplated. In *Silver Hill Duckling v Minister for Agriculture* ([1987] I.R. 289) the defendant ordered the plaintiffs

to slaughter their entire flock of ducks after an outbreak of avian influenza. The plaintiffs brought proceedings for damages and compensation under the Diseases of Animals Act 1966. In the course of the proceedings the defendants claimed privilege over a number of documents they were ordered to discover. O'Hanlon J. held that:

> "once litigation is apprehended or threatened, a party to such litigation is entitled to prepare his case, whether by means of communications passing between him and his legal advisors, or by means of communications passing between him and third parties, and to do so under the cloak of privilege."

He felt that this test was satisfied in this case once it became clear that what the plaintiffs were seeking in compensation was far in excess of what the defendants were prepared to pay. In a similar vein, in *Gallagher v Stanley*, O'Flaherty J. in the Supreme Court stated that "it is essential that litigation should be reasonably apprehended".

12.2.2.2 Dominant purpose

A document will only be protected by litigation privilege if it was prepared for the dominant purpose of the pending or contemplated litigation. The House of Lords established this dominant purpose test in *Waugh v The British Railway Board* ([1980] A.C. 521). Here the defendants employed the plaintiff's husband. He died in a railway accident. The plaintiff sought discovery of the defendant's internal reports concerning the accident. The defendant claimed these reports were privileged. The House of Lords held that for the reports to be privileged the dominant purpose for the preparation of the reports must have been the anticipated litigation. Here the reports were prepared for two equally important reasons, the anticipated litigation and to improve railway safety. Therefore the dominant purpose test was not satisfied and the reports were not privileged.

This test was endorsed in this jurisdiction in *Silverhill Duckling v Minister for Agriculture*. The Supreme Court also applied it in *Gallagher v Stanley*. Here the infant plaintiff claimed he had suffered severe personal injuries during his birth due to the negligence of the defendants. The plaintiff obtained an order for discovery and the defendants claimed that some documents were privileged, as they were prepared in contemplation of litigation. The documents were statements made by nurses who were on duty in the hospital at the relevant time. They were requested to make these statements by the matron of the hospital on the morning after the birth of the plaintiff. The matron claimed that the only reason she obtained the statements was that she anticipated litigation. The Supreme Court rejected this. O'Flaherty J. accepted that anticipated litigation might have been a reason, but he felt there were also other reasons. He felt that the matron also wanted to establish how the staff under her control had conducted themselves, which was important for the proper management and running of a hospital. Therefore, the statements failed the dominant purpose test and were not privileged.

12.2.3 Exceptions to legal professional privilege

There are four situations where the courts have been prepared to reject a claim of legal professional privilege. These are: (a) communications in furtherance of a crime or a fraud; (b) testamentary dispositions; (c) proceedings concerning the welfare of children; and (d) communications that help an accused establish his innocence.

12.2.3.1 Communications in furtherance of a crime or a fraud
The rationale for legal professional privilege is that it assists the administration of justice, so it is only right that communications in furtherance of a crime or fraud are not privileged. In *People (AG) v Coleman* ([1945] I.R. 237) the accused was charged with carrying out illegal abortions. The evidence against him included a piece of paper upon which he had written a list of names of people he had carried out abortions on. The trial judge considered that the accused had written the list because he wanted his solicitor to induce these people to commit perjury. Therefore, he held that the document was not privileged as it suggested the commission of a crime. The Court of Criminal Appeal upheld this decision.

This exception was extended in *Murphy v Kirwan* ([1993] 3 I.R. 501) to include conduct which is injurious to the interests of justice. Here the plaintiff sought specific performance of an alleged agreement. The defendant counter-claimed for damages on the grounds that the plaintiff's claim was frivolous, vexatious and was taken to prevent the defendant performing another agreement. The plaintiff's case was dismissed and the counter-claim was adjourned. The defendant then sought discovery of the legal advice the plaintiff had received in relation to the specific performance claim. The plaintiff argued that in the absence of an allegation of fraud this advice was privileged. In the Supreme Court Finlay C.J. held that "professional privilege cannot and must not be applied so as to be injurious to the interests of justice and to those in the administration of justice where persons have been guilty of conduct of moral turpitude or of dishonest conduct even though it may not be fraud." Therefore, the plaintiff could not claim privilege over the documents.

The Supreme Court was asked to further extend the exception in *Bula Ltd v Crowley (No.2)* ([1994] 2 I.R. 54). Here the first-named defendant was the receiver of the first-named plaintiff. The plaintiffs claimed he had been negligent in failing to follow certain legal advice he had obtained. They sought discovery of documents containing this legal advice. The Supreme Court held that these documents were privileged. This exception to the doctrine of legal professional privilege was restricted to cases where allegations of fraud, criminal conduct or conduct constituting an interference with the administration of justice were made. All of these allegations contain a clear element of moral turpitude. Here the plaintiffs were only claiming the defendant was negligent.

12.2.3.2 *Testamentary dispositions*
If the intention or capacity of a testator is challenged in legal proceedings the courts may be prepared to overlook the doctrine of legal professional privilege. As the client is dead there is arguably a less pressing need to maintain the privilege. O'Sullivan J. considered this issue in *Crawford v Treacy* ([1999] 2 I.R. 171). As the intention of the testator could be established by other means O'Sullivan J. was not prepared to disregard the privilege in this case. However, it is evident from his judgment that if the interests of justice required him to do so he would have ordered the disclosure of the documents.

12.2.3.3 *Proceedings concerning the welfare of children*
Proceedings involving the welfare of children are inquisitorial rather than adversarial in nature. Therefore, there are fewer reasons for strictly applying the doctrine of legal professional privilege. In *L (T) v L (V)* ([1996] I.F.L.R. 126) McGuinness J. was concerned with an application under s.3 of the Guardianship of Infants Act 1964. This Act requires the court to regard the welfare of the child as being of paramount importance. On that basis McGuinness J. was prepared to override the doctrine of legal professional privilege if it was necessary to establish what was in the interests of the welfare

of the child. However, she did not actually do so here as she held it to be unnecessary.

12.2.3.4 Communications that help an accused establish his innocence

It is not entirely clear if this is a valid exception to the doctrine of legal professional privilege. The courts have not considered the issue in this jurisdiction and there are conflicting judgments in the UK. In *R v Barton* ([1972] 2 All. E.R. 1192) the defendant was charged with fraudulent conversion and theft, alleged to have been committed in the course of his employment in a solicitor's office. He wanted certain documents from the office produced at his trial, which he claimed would help establish his innocence. A partner in the firm who had been subpoenaed argued that the documents were privileged. The court held that as the documents could help the accused establish his innocence, no privilege should attach.

However, the House of Lords reached a different conclusion in *R v Derby Magistrates' Court, Ex p. B* ([1996] 1 A.C. 487). Here the appellant had been acquitted of murder. Initially he admitted his guilt but later he claimed that his stepfather had killed the deceased and that he had taken part under duress. After his acquittal his stepfather was charged with the murder. Counsel for the stepfather wanted to get access to the appellant's communications with his solicitor to help establish his client's innocence. The House of Lords held that these documents were privileged.

12.2.4 Loss of legal professional privilege

Three situations where legal professional privilege can be lost will be considered: loss by waiver; disclosure of expert reports in personal injury actions; and where privileged documents are disclosed by inadvertence.

12.2.4.1 Waiver of privilege

The party entitled to claim privilege can waive it. This applies to all categories of privilege. With legal professional privilege the privilege belongs to the client, not the lawyer. Therefore, it is up to the client to decide if he wants to waive privilege. This can be done expressly or impliedly. For example, in *Mullen v Carty* (unreported, January 27, 1998) the appellant sued his former solicitors. He claimed they were negligent in their handling of previous litigation. In the High

Court a barrister briefed in the previous litigation gave evidence on behalf of the defendants. In the Supreme Court the appellant claimed this was in breach of the doctrine of legal professional privilege. The Supreme Court held that if a client puts in issue all the correspondence between the lawyer and the client he thereby impliedly waives the privilege of confidentiality.

Care needs to be taken if a party wants to waive privilege over part of a document only. In such circumstances it is possible for this to result in the whole document losing its privilege. For example, if a court considers that partial disclosure is unfair on the other side then it may decide that the whole document should be disclosed.

12.2.4.2 Disclosure of expert witness reports in personal injury actions

Before the introduction of S.I. No.391 of 1998, expert witness reports were covered by legal professional privilege. However, this rule requires that in personal injury actions any expert report that will be relied on during the trial must be disclosed to the other side beforehand.

12.2.4.3 Documents disclosed by inadvertence or by mistake

It is possible for prima facie privileged documents to lose their privilege because they were accidentally disclosed to the other side. The courts in this jurisdiction have not directly considered this controversial area; however, it has been considered on a number of occasions by the courts in the UK.

In *R v Tompkins* ((1977) 67 Cr. App. Rep. 1) the appellant was convicted of handling stolen goods. The goods included a stereo which the owner stated had a loose button. The appellant claimed the stereo was his and that it never had a loose button. Counsel for the prosecution then produced a note written by the appellant to his own counsel which stated that the button on his stereo had been loose and that he had glued it back on. The prosecution counsel had found this note on the courtroom floor. On appeal the court held that although the note was privileged from production it was admissible once it was in the possession of the prosecution.

This decision can be contrasted with *Guinness Peak Properties v Fitzroy Robinson Partnership* ([1987] 2 All E.R. 716). Here the defendant's solicitors inadvertently failed to claim privilege over a document that was clearly privileged. They tried to obtain an injunction to restrain the plaintiffs relying on it. The Court of Appeal held that in general once a document protected by privilege had been inspected it was too late for an injunction to be ordered. However, if the inspection was procured by fraud, or if the inspecting party realises he has only seen the document because of an obvious mistake, the court has the power to grant the injunction. Here the injunction was granted, as the plaintiffs must have known they were only permitted to see the document because of a mistake.

12.3 WITHOUT PREJUDICE COMMUNICATIONS

Communications between solicitors that attempt to settle proceedings are commonly described as "without prejudice" communications. This is because very often the phrase "without prejudice" appears at the top of the solicitor's letter. The reason why privilege attaches to such communications is that this encourages settlements. Without the rule any concession made during a negotiation would be admissible if the case went to court and if this were allowed fewer negotiations would take place.

To succeed in a claim of privilege under this heading it is vital that the party claiming the privilege show that the communication was made (a) in a genuine attempt to settle the dispute, and (b) with the intention that if the negotiations proved unsuccessful the communication could not be disclosed in any proceedings without the consent of the party. It is clear from the case law that the courts will examine documents headed "without prejudice" to see if they satisfy these requirements.

In *O'Flanagan v Ray-Ger Ltd* (unreported, April 28, 1983) the plaintiffs brought these proceedings to establish that the defendant company held property on trust for their benefit. They wanted to rely on a letter to that effect written by the defendant's solicitors. The defendant claimed the letter was privileged as it was headed "without prejudice". Costello J. held that this phrase does not possess "magic properties" which automatically make a letter privileged. Instead the court should examine the document to see if it was really made in a genuine attempt to settle the dispute. The letter in this case was written in reply to a request from the plaintiff for clarification as to whether she owned the land. The plaintiff had not threatened legal proceedings at that point. The letter was not written in an attempt to settle a dispute but was simply a statement as to the plaintiff's rights. Therefore it was not privileged.

In *Ryan v Connolly* ([2001] 2 I.L.R.M. 174) the plaintiff was claiming damages arising from a road traffic accident. The proceedings were instituted more than three years after the date of the accident. The defendant pleaded that the plaintiff's claim was statute-barred. The plaintiff claimed the defendant was estopped from relying on the Statute of Limitations Act 1957 because of certain statements made in "without prejudice" correspondence. In the Supreme Court Keane C.J. accepted that without prejudice privilege could not be applied in so inflexible a manner as to produce injustice. So if the defendant's correspondence had said that they would not raise the statute as a defence if the initiation of proceedings was deferred pending negotiations, the court could not be prevented from looking at such correspondence simply because it was headed without prejudice. On that basis the court was entitled to examine the correspondence. However, on examination the court could find nothing to indicate that the defendants would not raise the Statue of Limitations.

12.4 THE PRIVILEGE AGAINST SELF-INCRIMINATION

This privilege is also often referred to as "the right to silence". It can be regarded as being made up of a number of discrete entitlements. Here it will be considered under three sub-categories: (a) the right of an accused not to give evidence at his trial; (b) the right of a suspect to remain silent while being questioned; and (c) the right of witnesses (as distinct from the accused) not to answer any question which would incriminate them.

12.4.1 The right of an accused not to give evidence at his trial

In chapter 2 it was noted that although an accused is now competent to testify at his own trial he cannot be compelled to do so. Section 1 of the Criminal Justice Act 1924 provides that "the failure of any person charged with an offence…to give evidence shall not be made the subject of any comment by the prosecution."

In *Heaney v Ireland* Costello J. in the High Court felt that an accused's right not to have to give evidence was protected by Art.8.1 of the Constitution. In *People (DPP) v Finnerty* ([1999] 4 I.R. 364) Keane J. stated: "the exercise by an accused person of his right not to give evidence in his own defence cannot lead to any inferences adverse to him being drawn by the court and … in the case of the trial by jury, the jury must be expressly so advised by the trial judge".

12.4.2 The right of a suspect to remain silent while being questioned

The leading case on this issue is the Supreme Court decision in *Heaney v Ireland* ([1996] I.R. 580). Here the plaintiffs had been arrested under s.30 of the Offences Against the State Act 1939. Section 52 of the 1939 Act provides that where a person is detained under s.30 of the Act the gardaí can demand the person give a full account of their movements and actions during any specified period. If the person arrested fails to give such an account they are guilty of an offence, which can be punished by up to six months in prison. The plaintiffs were asked to account for their movements. They refused to do so and were convicted of an offence under s.52. In these proceedings they challenged the constitutionality of s.52 on the basis that it infringed, *inter alia*, the constitutionally guaranteed right to silence. In the High Court Costello J. accepted that a citizen's right to a fair trial under Art.38.1 of the Constitution protected a suspect's right to silence. However, he held that this was not an absolute right and that the restriction set out in s.52 was a proportionate restriction on that right and therefore it was constitutional.

The Supreme Court also upheld the constitutionality of the provision. They did so, however, on a different basis. O'Flaherty J. gave the judgment of the court. He began by stating that: "Where a person is totally innocent of any wrongdoing as regards his movements, it would require a strong attachment to one's apparent constitutional rights not to give such an account when asked pursuant to a statutory requirement." He then held that a suspect's right to silence was a corollary of his right to freedom of expression protected by Art.40.6 of the Constitution. He noted that a citizen's freedom of expression was subject to public order and morality. He stated that these limitations also applied to a suspect's right of silence. Therefore, he held that the State was entitled to encroach on the right of the citizen to remain silent in pursuit of its entitlement to maintain peace and order. But in this pursuit the constitutional rights of the citizen must be affected as little as possible. Therefore, the question for the court was "whether the restriction which s.52 places on the right to silence is any greater than is necessary having regard to the disorder against which the State is attempting to protect the public". The court concluded that here, because of the exceptional nature of s.52, the restriction was proportionate and therefore s.52 was constitutional.

The plaintiffs then took Ireland to the European Court of Human Rights. Here it was held that there had been a breach of their right to a fair trial under Art.6 of the Convention. The court held that:

> "the 'degree of compulsion', imposed on the applicants by the application of section 52 of the 1939 Act with a view to compelling them to provide information relating to charges against them under that Act, in effect, destroyed the very essence of their privilege against self-incrimination and their right to remain silent."

12.4.2.1 Adverse inferences from silence

Several recent statutes permit adverse inferences to be drawn from an accused's decision to remain silent after he has been arrested. Sections 18 and 19 of the Criminal Justice Act 1984 permit adverse inferences to be drawn from an accused's failure to explain his possession of a particular object (s.18) or his presence at a particular place (s.19) when asked to do so by the gardaí. Section 3 of the Criminal Justice (Forensic Evidence) Act 1990 permits adverse inferences to be drawn from an accused's refusal to provide samples for DNA testing. Section 7 of the Criminal Justice (Drug Trafficking) Act 1996 and s.5 of the Offences Against the State (Amendment) Act 1998 both provide that adverse inferences can be drawn from an accused's failure to mention any fact while in custody which he later relies on for his defence.

In *Rock v Ireland* ([1997] 3 I.R. 484) the constitutionality of ss.18 and 19 of the 1984 Act were considered. The applicant claimed they infringed his constitutionally guaranteed right to silence. In contrast to *Heaney* the Supreme Court appeared to accept the High Court's view that Art.38.1 of the Constitution protected the accused's right to silence. The court noted that ss.18 and 19 restricted this right. However, the right was not absolute so the question for the court was whether the legislature's restriction of this right was proportionate. In deciding that the interference was proportionate the court took into account that an inference could not form the basis of a conviction in the absence of other evidence and that an inference adverse to the accused could only be drawn where the court deemed it proper to do so.

It is important to note that adverse inferences can only be drawn if permitted by statute. The Supreme Court clearly established this point in *People (DPP) v Finnerty* ([1999] 4 I.R. 364). Here the appellant was charged with rape. At his trial he disputed the complainant's version of events. During cross-examination it was put to him that he had not mentioned his version of events to the gardaí while detained under s.4 of the Criminal Justice Act 1984 and that he had in fact refused to answer their questions. He was convicted. He appealed his conviction on the basis that the prosecution should not have been permitted to highlight to the jury his silence while in garda custody. The Court of Criminal Appeal held that there had been no breach of his right to silence. However, the Supreme Court disagreed. Keane J. gave the unanimous judgment. He began by noting that at common law a suspect was entitled not to answer any questions and that the gardaí had to inform him of this right when cautioning him. This right was not altered by the 1984 Act. In ss.18 and 19 of the 1984 Act the Oireachtas had specifically allowed adverse inferences to be drawn but only in limited circumstances. The Act did not contain any general provision allowing adverse inferences to be drawn. This meant that no "general abridgment of the right to silence was intended to be effected where a person declined to answer questions put to him by the gardaí". Therefore he held that "[u]nder no circumstances should any cross-examination by the prosecution as to the refusal of the defendant during the course of his detention to answer any questions be permitted."

The European Court of Human Rights has considered adverse-inference-drawing legislation on a number of occasions. In *Murray v UK* ((1996) 22 E.H.R.R. 29) the court was prepared to accept that the right to silence was not absolute and that adverse-inference-drawing legislation could be compatible with the convention in certain circumstances. It held that:

> "The national court cannot conclude that the accused is guilty merely because he chooses to remain silent. It is only if the evidence against the accused 'calls' for an explanation which the accused ought to be in a position to give that a failure to give an explanation 'may as a matter of common sense allow the drawing of an inference that there is no explanation and that the accused is guilty'."

Here the evidence did call for an explanation. However, the court went on to hold that there had been a breach of Art.6 as the applicant had been denied access to a solicitor for the first 48 hours of his detention. The court held that it was extremely important for a suspect who has been arrested under adverse-inference-drawing legislation to get access to legal advice at the initial stages of police interrogation.

Similarly, in *Averill v UK* ((2001) 31 E.H.R.R. 839) the court felt that the fact that the applicant had been denied access to his solicitor for the first 24 hours of his detention was significant in determining whether adverse inferences should have been drawn. It stated: "access to a lawyer should have been guaranteed to the applicant before his interrogation began". Ultimately, however, the court held that his right to a fair trial had not been breached. There was a considerable amount of other evidence, which required an explanation. He had been caught near the incident and incriminating fibres were discovered on his clothes.

In *Condron v UK* ((2001) 21 E.H.R.R. 1) the applicants were drug addicts. They were advised by their solicitor to remain silent during police questioning as he considered they were unfit to answer questions. The trial judge led the jury to believe they could still draw adverse inferences from their silence even though the explanation for their silence was plausible. The European Court of Human Rights held that this breached the applicants' right to a fair trial.

12.4.3 The right of witnesses not to answer any question which would incriminate them

The leading case in this area is *Re National Irish Bank (No.1)* ([1999] 3 I.R. 145). Here two inspectors were appointed by the High Court under the Companies Act 1990 to inspect certain matters at National Irish Bank. They applied for directions from the High Court as to whether persons from whom they sought information, documents or evidence could refuse to provide documents or answer questions on the ground that the documents or answers might tend to incriminate them. Section 10 of the 1990 Act requires officers and agents of a company being investigated and other persons in possession of relevant information to co-operate with the inspectors and to produce documents and answer questions. Section 18 of the 1990 Act provides that an answer given by a person "may be used in evidence against him". In the High Court Shanley J. was satisfied that s.10 abrogated a person's privilege against self-incrimination. However, he held that in accordance with the principles laid down in *Heaney* the restriction was proportionate. He stated:

"It is, of course, a legitimate objective of the State, and entirely in the public interest, to lay bare frauds and dishonest stratagems, and where the only means of effectively achieving such an objective is to provide an investigative procedure without a right to silence (as in the instant case) then one can properly assert that the restrictions imposed by s.10 on the right to silence are no greater than is necessary to enable the State to fulfil its constitutional obligations".

The Supreme Court upheld this decision. In the High Court Shanley J. did not consider whether answers compelled under s.10 could be admissible in any subsequent criminal trial. However, in the Supreme Court Barrington J. held they were not.

12.5 JOURNALISTIC PRIVILEGE

In *Re Kevin O'Kelly* ((1974) 108 I.L.T.R. 97) the Supreme Court rejected a claim of privilege made by a journalist over his sources. However, this decision can be contrasted with *Burke v Central Independent Television plc* ([1994] 2 I.R. 61). Here the plaintiffs claimed damages for libel arising out of a television programme broadcast by the defendant. In the programme it was alleged that premises owned by one of the plaintiffs was the financial nerve centre of the IRA. The plaintiffs obtained an order for discovery. The defendants objected to producing certain documents which would lead to the identification of its sources as the life of those sources would be put at risk if their identities became known. The Supreme Court upheld the defendant's claim of privilege as the constitutional right to life of the sources took precedence over the plaintiffs' right to their good name.

12.6 INFORMER PRIVILEGE

Since *AG v Briant* ((1846) 15 M. & W. 169) the Irish courts have accepted that privilege can be claimed in respect of the identities of informers. The reason was that if their identities were revealed they would be in danger and if no privilege existed there would be fewer informers, which would make crime detection more difficult. Initially informer privilege only applied to police informers. However, in *D v NSPCC* ([1978] A.C. 171) the House of Lords extended this privilege to cover communications made to the National Society for the Prevention of Cruelty to Children in relation to alleged child abuse.

This decision was approved in Ireland in a number of cases. In *Director of Consumer Affairs v Sugar Distributors Ltd* ([1991] 1 I.R. 225) Costello J. held that a complaint made by a company to the plaintiff that the defendants had breached restrictive practice legislation was privileged. In *Goodman International v Hamilton (No.3)* ([1993] 3 I.R. 320) Geoghegan J. held that TDs could rely on informer privilege to protect the identity of their sources. The court felt that it was important that matters of public interest could be brought to the attention of public representatives in confidence.

12.7 MARITAL PRIVILEGE

This is a privilege enjoyed by a husband and wife not to disclose any communications made by the other spouse during their marriage. In relation to civil proceedings it originated in the Evidence (Amendment) Act 1853. This Act did not apply to criminal proceedings, as originally spouses were not competent or compellable in such proceedings. This privilege was abolished by the Criminal Evidence Act 1992 which made a spouse of an accused competent to testify on behalf of the prosecution and compellable in certain limited circumstances. However, s.26 of the 1992 Act states: "nothing in this Act shall affect the right of a spouse to marital privacy".

12.8 SACERDOTAL PRIVILEGE

In *Cook v Carroll* ([1945] I.R. 515) the court had to determine whether a priest who refused to testify about a conversation he had with the defendant was guilty of contempt of court. Gavan-Duffy J. held that in order for the conversation to be privileged four conditions must be satisfied:

1. The communications must originate in the *confidence* that they will not be disclosed;
2. This element of *confidentiality must be essential* to the full and satisfactory maintenance of the relation;
3. The *relation* must be one which in the opinion of the community ought to be sedulously *fostered*; and
4. The *injury* which would enure to the relation by the disclosure of the communications must be *greater*

than the benefit thereby gained for the correct disposal of litigation.

Here the court held that the four conditions were satisfied and therefore the communication was privileged.

In *Johnston v Church of Scientology* (unreported, April 30, 1999) Geoghegan J. expressed reservations about this judgment. Here the plaintiff claimed she had been brainwashed by the defendants. She sought disclosure of "counselling notes" which had been made during "spiritual practices" of scientology called "auditing" and "training". The defendant claimed these sessions were confidential and that the notes were privileged. They compared these sessions to a Catholic going to confession. The court rejected this analogy. The court was prepared to accept that there could be a counsellor privilege, *e.g.* if a priest counselled a parishioner. However, the person who had been counselled could waive this privilege and if it applied here the plaintiff was clearly waiving it.

12.9 PUBLIC PRIVILEGE

This is a privilege which can be claimed by an organ of the State in certain circumstances. Traditionally at common law the English courts had recognised a privilege known as "crown privilege". In *Leen v President of the Executive Council* ([1925] I.R. 456) Meredith J. in the High Court held that this privilege survived the establishment of the Free State although he preferred to describe it as a public interest privilege.

Initially the courts in both jurisdictions were not prepared to go behind what was known as a ministerial certificate. This was a statement by the relevant minister that the disclosure of a class of documents would be against the public interest. The courts would accept this certificate without question and would refuse the disclosure sought. However, the House of Lords in *Conway v Rimmer* ([1968] A.C. 910) restricted the application of this rule. They held that a court should normally endorse a Minister's decision unless: (a) it was not shown to have been made in good faith; (b) it was unreasonable; or (c) it was based on a misunderstanding of the issues.

Kenny J. followed this approach in the High Court in *Murphy v Dublin Corporation* ([1972] I.R. 215). Here the defendant made a compulsory purchase order of land owned by the plaintiff. The plaintiff objected to this order and the Minister for Local Government appointed an inspector to carry out an enquiry into the issue. The inspector produced a report and the Minister claimed this report was privileged. Applying the above test Kenny J. held that the report was privileged. The Supreme Court overturned this decision. Walsh J. rejected the view that the Minister could decide if the documents should be produced. Instead he held that under the Constitution the judiciary are responsible for the administration of justice and the power to compel the production of evidence is an inherent part of the administration of justice. Therefore he held that the court and not the Minister should decide if in the public interest the documents should be disclosed. He accepted that it might be rare for a court, after its own examination, to arrive at a different conclusion from that expressed by the Minister, but that was far removed from accepting, without question, the judgment of the Minister.

Walsh J. concluded that once a document is relevant the burden of satisfying the court that it should not be disclosed rests on the party claiming the privilege and they must satisfy this burden in respect of each document. This means that:

> "there can be no documents which may be withheld from production simply because they belong to a particular class of documents. Each document must be decided upon having regard to the considerations which apply to that particular document and its contents."

The Supreme Court was invited to overturn their decision in *Murphy* in *Ambiorix Limited v Minister for the Environment* ([1992] 1 I.R. 277). The defendants appealed a High Court order, which required them to discover certain documents. They argued that the documents, which emanated from a senior level of the public service, related to the formulation of policy and legislative proposals, and were intended for ministerial consideration, belonged to a class of documents which were absolutely privileged and which did not require to be examined by a trial judge. The Supreme Court unanimously rejected this argument. Finlay C.J. began by noting that the defendant was asking the Supreme Court to approve several English decisions that were in conflict with *Murphy*. He felt that this argument was flawed because it ignored the "fundamental constitutional origin" of *Murphy*. He then summarised the principles laid down in Murphy as follows:

"1. Under the Constitution the administration of justice is committed solely to the judiciary by the exercise of their powers in the courts set up under the Constitution.

2. Power to compel the production of evidence (which, of course, includes a power to compel the production of documents) is an inherent part of that judicial power and is part of the ultimate safeguard of justice in the State.

3. Where a conflict arises during the exercise of the judicial power between the aspect of public interest involved in the production of evidence and the aspect of public interest involved in the confidentiality or exemption from production of documents pertaining to the exercise of the executive powers of the State, it is the judicial power which will decide which public interest shall prevail.

4. The duty of the judicial power to make that decision does not mean that there is any priority or preference for the production of evidence over other public interests, such as the security of the State or the efficient discharge of the functions of the executive organ of the Government.

5. It is for the judicial power to choose the evidence upon which it might act in any individual case in order to reach that decision."

The Chief Justice then went on to say that these principles led to certain conclusions applicable to a claim of privilege by the executive:

"(a) The executive cannot prevent the judicial power from examining documents which are relevant to an issue in a civil trial for the purpose of deciding whether they must be produced.

(b) There is no obligation on the judicial power to examine any particular document before deciding that it is exempt from production, and it can and will in many instances uphold a claim of privilege in respect of a document merely on the basis of a description of its nature and contents which it (the judicial power) accepts.

(c) There cannot, accordingly, be a general applicable class
      or category of documents exempted from production
      by reason of the rank in the public service of the per-
      son creating them, or of the position of the individual
      body intended to use them."

From these decisions it is possible to work out the approach a judge
should adopt to determine if public interest privilege applies to a
document. He should weigh up the public interest in the administration
of justice (which favours disclosure) against the public interest being
put forward in favour of non-disclosure. In determining what weight
to attach to the first public interest the key issue according to Keane
J. in *Breathnach v Ireland (No.3)* ([1993] 2 I.R. 458) is "to what
extent, if any, the relevant documents may advance the plaintiff's
case or damage the defendants' case or fairly lead to an enquiry
which may have either of those consequences".

There could be any number of public interests put forward in
favour of non-disclosure. It would be nearly impossible to set out a
comprehensive list. For example, in *Breathnach* Keane J. accepted
that there was a public interest in the prevention and prosecution of
crime. Here the plaintiff's conviction for armed robbery was
overturned by the Court of Criminal Appeal. He then brought these
proceedings claiming damages for, *inter alia*, malicious prosecution.
He obtained an order of discovery against the DPP of comm–
unications from the gardaí concerning his arrest, detention and
interrogation. The defendants discovered numerous documents but
claimed privilege over them. Keane J. was satisfied that to determine
whether the documents were privileged he had to weigh the
competing public interests. He held that in the particular
circumstances of this case (it was a claim for malicious prosecution
after a criminal conviction had been quashed) the public interest in
the administration of justice outweighed the public interest in the
prevention and prosecution of crime. Therefore, he examined the
documents and ordered that some of them were not privileged.

In *Murphy* Walsh J. gave the example of the security of the
State. He declared:

"It is clear that, when the vital interests of the State (such
as the security of the State) may be adversely affected by
disclosure or production of a document, greater harm may

be caused by ordering rather than refusing disclosure or production of the document. In such a case the courts would refuse the order".

In *Director of Consumer Affairs v Sugar Distributors Ltd* ([1991] 1 I.R. 225) the court relied on the public interest in the proper functioning of the public service to uphold the plaintiff's claim of privilege.

Index